Widowed Without Warning

Widowed Without Warning

◆

Joanne Shortley-Lalonde

Writer's Showcase
San Jose New York Lincoln Shanghai

Writer's Showcase
an imprint of iUniverse.com, Inc.

For information address:
iUniverse.com, Inc.
5220 S 16th, Ste. 200
Lincoln, NE 68512
www.iuniverse.com

ISBN: 0-595-16387-4

Printed in the United States of America

To Steve Shortley,
I am who I am
Because you loved me…

I also wish to dedicate this book to
Lisa and Dan,
My heart and my soul.
We stood huddled together and
Weathered the storm
Until the rainbow appeared again.
And also
To all the families of the 427
Plane crash.
On September 8, 1994
When they announced that USAir flight 427 had
"NO SURVIVORS,"
They were wrong.
We are the survivors.

Epigraph

◆

For everything there is a season and a time for every
purpose under heaven

A time to plant and a time to reap
A time to laugh and a time to weep
A time for silence and a time to speak
A time to give and a time to take
A time to love and a time to hate
A time to embrace and a time to refrain
A time to scatter stones and
A time to gather them together
A time to be born and a time to die
A time for war and a time for peace
Ecclesiastes 3:19

Contents

◆

(The Cover)

The Tree

———————— ◆ ————————

Two years after my husband died, I was
Driving along a country road
Deep in thought.
Suddenly I realized I was lost.
As I turned my car around in the middle of nowhere,
I came face to face with a huge tree.
It was half dead
Half alive.
I sat in my car staring at this remarkable looking tree.
One half was full of bright green bushy leaves;
the other half had bare almost dead branches.
"That is me!"
I told myself.
That is exactly how I feel without Steve.
Half dead…half alive.

Acknowledgements

◆

I
Wish to thank
My entire family,
Especially my sister Donna and my brother Mike,
My cousin Carol and my friend Leenie,
And all of my special friends who
With their patience and love
Helped us through the painful times.
Special thanks to my second Prince Charming,
Jean-Pierre (JP) Lalonde
And my
New three daughters, Melinda, Karen and Valerie
For making
Me "normal" again…

Introduction

◆

(Published in the Pittsburgh Post-Gazette 9-9-96)
On September 8, 1994, my husband, Stephen M. Shortley, a 37-year-old handsome, kind and intelligent man with twinkling brown eyes, and a great sense of humor, was killed in an airplane crash in Pittsburgh. USAir flight 427. All 132 people aboard died. It was the worst tragedy my family and I had ever experienced. It was an airline disaster that will be remembered in Pittsburgh for many years and I was smack right in the middle of it.

They say the first year of grief is the hardest. I think the second year is equally as hard, if not harder.

The first year you are in complete shock, mass confusion, and deep depression. You are immediately expected to deal with all of the responsibilities that you once shared with your spouse: the children, the house, the car, and the finances. The future is now part of the past. How can you possibly think about a future once full of hopes and dreams, when every moment is spent missing, yearning, and grieving the one you've lost?

Because the airplane crash was so public, and the devastation so severe, we had to deal with a situation that was not your normal death. When a spouse or loved one leaves for work and just doesn't come home, there aren't any last words, any quick questions to ask, no preparing, no finalities and in our case no bodies to say good-bye to. There was never any closure.

We were expected to just accept. We were all thrown into a tornado of emotions and wanted desperately to come out feeling normal again.

I was not prepared for widowhood. One minute we were a happy "Donna Reed" family, the next minute I was wearing a black suit, walking down the aisle of a completely filled church, all sympathetic eyes, including the media, following my every step, one child at each side, and suddenly I felt a connection with Jackie Kennedy. Be strong, hold that head high, make him proud. I promised myself I would collapse after the funeral.

The first year I was under a protective shield of denial. Maybe this was a big mistake. Maybe he really wasn't on that plane. He tripped and fell in Chicago, hit his head and has amnesia. Every night I went to bed praying that soon someone would awaken me from this awful nightmare. But nobody ever did. It was very real. I was now alone in a world full of people.

Welcome to Widowhood.

The second year the numbness begins to wear off and realization sets in. I needed to resign myself with a long breathless sigh that he really was not coming home.

When you are suddenly widowed, everything that used to be shared by two now becomes the responsibility for one. There was no time to adjust or prepare for single parenthood. It is a struggle to just get out of bed each morning knowing the pain exceeds your every moment, but there are children to feed, dishes to wipe, clothes to wash, papers to sign, and bills to be paid. So you push through the grief with the force of a windstorm. Life becomes one exhausting chore.

You are tired of dealing with the problems of everyday life. You are tired of being afraid of making decisions that can affect you and your children forever. You are tired of worrying about what you would do if the water heater broke, or the furnace stopped working in the middle of the night in the middle of a snowstorm. What if the gutters leak or the clothes dryer vent comes off again? He is no longer there to be your hero. You are tired of searching for appliance manuals not knowing where he placed them and not being able to pick up the telephone and ask him. There is no direct line to heaven.

You are tired of not being a full family at restaurants, amusement parks, holiday dinners, weddings, vacation spots, and school functions. You are tired of trying to remember what it was like kissing him and being held by him. Just looking across the living room where he used to sit is painfully empty. You are tired of not being part of a couple in a couple's world. You are tired of turning your head away from loving couples holding hands at the mall, and worse yet is seeing husbands and wives argue unnecessarily over unimportant issues, you just want to shake them and tell them your tragic story. You are tired of the loneliness.

You are tired of wives who complain about their husbands' dirty socks and the fact that they are sick of cooking dinner every night. And then there are those who insensitively brag about the beautiful birthday present or the bouquet of roses they received for Valentines Day. You are tired of having to remember a time when you also were presented with red roses. And you would love to pick up his dirty socks again.

Most of the second year is spent being tired.

In the second year everyone assumes you are fine. The phone calls stop, offers to help stop, and unfortunately for some, friendships stop. No one wants to be around unhappy grieving people. Those who have never experienced a tragic death are impatient with your recovery. They think it is just a matter of saying, "Get on with it!" One thing I have learned is that everyone grieves differently. There is no set time limit on pain. Even if you appear to be doing fine on the outside, your inside is still a mass of uncertainty.

People commend me on my strength. They don't see me at the cemetery sitting alone on top of my husband's grave staring at his name wondering why this tragedy happened to us. Everyone tries to be helpful insisting that life must go on. And I know they are right. But they don't have the solution as to how to get rid of the pain. No one does. No one can. I knew from day one the only thing that would help me besides my husband's miraculous return...was time. And time does help. I just wanted to fast forward through life like a VCR.

Then comes the day when you decide it is time to go forward without him. It is what he would want you to do. You begin to make little plans, redecorate the bedroom, change your hairstyle, do some traveling, and meet new people. You have to learn how to live your life all over again. You have to come to terms with the fact that although it will never be the same, it will only be as good as you make it. You find that you can laugh again. Life does go on. Whether you want it to or not.

You wonder if you will ever have love again, afraid to trust. When you do meet someone, you risk your heart with major concerns. You will always be afraid of losing...again. Of hurting...again. But you learn that without the risk, you lose the opportunity of smelling the roses. And star filled skies at night just aren't the same unless they are shared.

I am fortunate in that I have a wonderful family and terrific friends. However, I knew that no matter how hard they tried; they could not possibly know how I felt. Their lives were not altered on a daily basis like my children's and mine. Our home was no longer the same. Everywhere we looked, we were reminded of the vacancy.

So I sought out support from the other surviving spouses from the airplane crash. Some of my closest friends now are Flight 427 family members. We have been there for one another at all hours of the night, listening, and encouraging, sharing opinions and advice, laughing and crying. We have been together for birthdays, anniversaries, memorial services, and some holidays. We have lunches, dinners and picnics. Some of us have even traveled together. We are family now. We are our strongest support. When the T.W.A. 800 crashed, many of us lived through our crash all over again. Some of us wanted to meet with those families and warn them, help them. Our hearts broke right along with theirs. We knew it all too well.

One night, nine of us young widows decided we needed to start going out. We went to a place where they have a sing-a-long to double piano players. We were singing and laughing and having an enjoyable time. Out of the blue, the piano player began playing Billy Joel's "Only the Good Die Young." Suddenly, each one of us stopped, looked around the table, tears forming in our eyes. We knew what each of us was thinking. All of our husbands were good and they all died young. Without skipping a beat and amidst the room full of strangers singing loudly and clapping to Billy's tune, the nine of us choked back our emotions, raised our glasses in the air and quietly toasted our husbands. Some of us had tears, some quivering smiles; some just shrugged shoulders and shook their heads. It never leaves us. Somehow no matter how hard we try to go on, no matter what we do, no matter where we go, there are reminders of what we have lost, what we no longer have.

FAIRY TALES AND CASTLES

◆

Cinderella finds herself all alone in the palace, and the Kingdom as she once knew and loved will never ever be the same. For now she is a Widow.

Once upon a time in the fairy tale land of happily ever after, Cinderella met her Prince. She married him for better or worse, in sickness and in health, for richer or poorer, and with dreamy lovelorn eyes she dutifully recited, "Till death do we part."

Under most normal circumstances, the "Till death do we part" segment of this fairy tale should not occur for many years. There are dreams to come true, children to be raised, traveling to be experienced, and someday hopefully, grandchildren to spoil.

But for some fluke of a reason, some mean unexplainable jolt through the heart, Cinderella finds herself all alone in the palace, and the Kingdom as she once knew and loved will never ever be the same. For now she is a Widow.

I always believed in happy fairy tales endings. I silently wished upon shooting stars, tossed pennies into fountains, and trusted my guardian angel to guide me through the darkest night. I always lived by the law "If you do good things…good things will return in triple."

I married my high school sweetheart and was under the impression that we would grow old together, gracefully and lovingly, reaping the benefits of the long awaited retirement. We had a special love and respect for one another that was greater than anything on this earth. After twenty years of marriage, and two beautiful children, we continued to hold hands when we walked. We winked, flirted and smiled at one another across a crowded room. We always knew that no matter what happened in our lives, as long as we had each other, we could get through anything. He was my best friend. He was my pillar of strength. He was half of me. I thought my husband was infallible. He rarely complained about aches and pains and because he was seldom sick; he never missed work. He was strong and healthy and in the prime of his career. He was only thirty-seven years old. People aren't supposed to die when they are only thirty-seven years old!

On that fateful Thursday in September of 1994, at approximately 3:30 p.m., Steve called me from the Chicago airport. Because his business meeting had finished early, he changed his flight. Instead of returning to Pittsburgh at nine o'clock that evening, he would be home a little after seven. Of course I was delighted that he would be home earlier than I expected. We could go out to dinner and talk about our day.

However, on a clear sunny evening, USAir flight 427 fell from the sky killing all 132 people. My husband, Stephen M. Shortley, father of Lisa and Daniel, son of Edward and Eleanor, brother of Jim, David and Michael, unfortunately picked the wrong flight. We never saw or heard him again. I became a widow without warning.

There are some events of that evening that will always remain foggy, but as time passes, I am able to recollect certain occurrences. After the telephone call with Steve that afternoon, I realized I had forgotten to ask him which airline he would be flying home on. He used several different airlines depending on which one arrived home the earliest. I only remember him saying he would be home "a little after 7:00 p.m." I liked knowing the flight number because I could call the 800 number to see what time the plane landed and know exactly what time he would be walking through the door. It would take him less than an hour to be home if the plane landed on time.

At about 8:05 p.m., I turned on the television set and saw a special news report flashing on the screen. As I always do when I see a "Special News Report," I instantly took inventory of my family. Both of my teenage children were home, but my husband wasn't. So I looked at the television and said, "Please don't be an airplane crash."

The newscaster then somberly announced, "There was an airplane crash near Pittsburgh this evening, a little after seven o'clock."

Steve's words echoed in my mind, *"I'll be home a little after seven."* I stopped breathing and whispered to myself, "Please don't be from Chicago…" I thought I might be over-reacting for a second. I mean, what are the chances that of all of the thousands of airplanes that fly, this one that crashed would be the one my husband was on. Much to my dismay, I heard the words quickly exit the newsman's mouth.

"There have been reports that the plane that crashed was coming into Pittsburgh from Chicago…" I lost the feeling in both of my legs and fell to the floor in my bedroom.

I screamed for both of my children. Thinking I had dropped something, they ran into my bedroom concerned for my safety. I pointed to the television and with a shaken voice said, "There was a plane crash in Pittsburgh and I think your dad might have been on it."

Terrified, the three of us stood huddled in a circle in front of the television set holding onto one another for dear life. This would be the beginning of the end of life, as we had known it. We would never ever have that feeling of security of our full family again. The four of us were now three.

I quickly telephoned my sister and my cousin, who is my best friend, and told them of my fears and asked them to come immediately to my home. A few minutes later my telephone rang. I prayed it was Steve telling me he was on his way home from the airport. It wasn't. The nervous voice on the other end of the line was his mother. How do you tell a woman that you think her son was on the airplane that just crashed? She called because she knew Steve was in Chicago and that he was coming home that night. I suggested that she call her other two sons and come to our house also. Within thirty minutes, my house was filled with our family and we sat vigil waiting to hear some kind of confirmation as to whether or not he was on that dreadful flight.

We paced in front of the television set watching the news hearing over and over again that there were no survivors. My sister called the telephone number that was flashing on the screen all evening trying to get some sort of information. Most of the time she would receive a busy signal. Several times I would walk past her and hear her calm but stern voice demanding to know if "Stephen Shortley" was on flight 427. I was grateful that she was the one dealing with the airlines and not me.

Still not believing my husband would be one of the victims, I hung onto the hope that any minute he would walk through our front door wondering why everyone was here and we would all have a big laugh and he would tell me once again how I worry too much. Everyone could go home and resume their lives as though nothing happened. Oh, how I prayed for that little scenario.

But then as minutes turned into hours and the airlines would not confirm if he was on flight 427, and I had not heard from him, I was pretty certain if he were alive, he would have called me by now. He was one of the most considerate men I knew. He would call me from work when he was more than fifteen minutes late for dinner. By the third hour, I remember holding onto my cousin Carol's hand telling her that I knew he was on that plane. Being my best friend, she and I have been through everything together in our lives. I told her that if by some miracle Steve did come home, I would never allow him out of my sight again.

I tried to bargain with God. I swore I would never nag my husband ever again about anything. I would go to church every Sunday without failure no matter what. I promised that if God allowed him to come home safely, I would demand he quit and look for a job with another company that did not require so much traveling. I never wanted to go through this again!

At one point, we finally reached someone from the airlines who said that my husband did change to flight 427 but he was a "no show." Everyone in the house cheered. My eighteen-year-old daughter wrapped a blanket around her shoulders to protect her from the cold night air and stood outside in the dark street waiting for his red car. I knew everyone was going to be extremely dejected. Didn't they listen to me? He would have called me. He knew I was a worrier. He would have jumped over cars and ran to a public telephone to call me.

I telephoned my older brother in Las Vegas. Earlier in the evening, his wife heard the news of a plane crashing in Pittsburgh and she called us to make sure we were all okay. They of course were in shock when we told them there was a chance that Steve was on the airplane. Their whole family was sitting together waiting for some word from us.

I remember telling my brother, "Mike, I'm too young to be a widow! I know he was on that plane and no one here will listen to me."

Not knowing what to say just yet, in his warm comforting way he replied,

"Oh Jo, you can't be a widow…your just a kid!" Since both of our parents were already dead, he and I and our sister Donna were very close and we both knew it was only going to be a matter of time before he and his family would be headed back to Pittsburgh to comfort us in person.

I rejoined the rest of the group in the family room and sat on top of the cold-cemented raised hearth in front of the fireplace glancing at everyone around the room. Their eyes were still glued to the television listening intently to the news of "USAir Flight 427. No survivors. No survivors." My daughter had finally come in from the chilled night and sat there quietly. My son nervously paced back and forth.

Finally at 2:45 a.m. after almost eight hours of painful waiting, my sister and Steve's brother entered the family room with a look upon their faces that will remain in my memory for the rest of my life. They had just spoken with the airlines. Quietly my sister whispered the words no one wanted to hear.

"*He was on the plane.*" She couldn't even look straight at me when she spoke. She stared straight ahead towards no one. Just looking at the wall. I watched as the words flowed out of her mouth like something out of a time warp machine. Shock began to set in as my ears deafened from the sounds around me. I actually felt sorry for her having to be the bearer of the bad news. I instinctively knew my husband was on that flight, but now hearing the actual words was like a dagger through my heart.

Almost instantly, a protective shield formed around me and I wanted no one to come near me. I didn't cry. I couldn't cry. I was in shock. I was in disbelief. I waited for my alarm clock to awaken me from this dreadful nightmare. Around me, I heard weeping and moaning and words of denial. I watched as my brother-in-law held my sister as she cried on his shoulder and my cousin's husband held her and my son and his girlfriend cried together and my daughter's boyfriend held onto her as she sobbed like a baby. I realized at that moment that the only person I wanted to comfort me and hold me was not there. I would have to become accustomed to standing alone. I looked over at my mother-in-law sitting alone on the chair across from me. She had the same look of disbelief that was probably on my face. Both of Steve's brother's were wiping their tears, each at her side standing there with long sorrowful faces. I slowly walked over to my mother-in-law and put my arms around her. I don't think she wanted anyone either. But I thought it was the right thing to do at the time.

After a few minutes, I calmly walked into the kitchen and my sister handed me the telephone. It was my brother and my nephew from Las Vegas. I instinctively took the telephone in my hand and slowly raised it to my ear. When I heard their low crackling voices telling me they didn't know quite what to say, it was as though someone threw ice water in my face and awoke me from a coma. Hearing them somehow made it seem real. All at once, I screamed blood-curdling screams. I remember not having any control over this. The screaming just flew out of my mouth. I heard my sister say, "Let her go, it's the first time she was able to cry and show some sort of reaction." My brother tried to comfort me by assuring me that they would be in Pittsburgh the next day.

THE ACCIDENT

◆

I had no clue this accident was going to be as huge as it was.

Most everything else is a blur. Around four o'clock in the morning everyone decided to go home to their own houses. We were all completely drained and exhausted. I think I rested in my bed for about five minutes with my daughter next to me. Neither one of us could sleep. Finally she went into her own room and I must have dozed off for a few minutes. I woke up; I felt the empty side of the bed, realized that the night before was not a bad dream, panicked and immediately telephoned my sister crying to her. She said they would be back over within an hour.

I could not have gotten through this tragedy without my sister, her husband, my family and several close friends. I was totally lost and unable to do even the simplest things. My sister became my shadow, my protector, and my right and left arm. I always tell her she was the wind beneath my wings. Without her wind I would never have had the ability to fly again. Her husband Larry, who had the patience of an angel, became our chauffeur because I was unable to drive. He lost one of his best buddies when Steve died and he couldn't even mourn his death around me. He and the rest of my family needed to place their grief on the shelf in order to help us get through this traumatic time.

All of us were still in a daze from a mixture of shock and sleep deprivation. By 8:00 a.m., my sister and my cousin were back in my house offering to help place the dreadful telephone calls. I remember thinking of the many people we knew who watched the news about the plane crash and went to bed unaware that Steve was one of the victims. We would need to call the rest of our family, his boss, and all of our friends. A million things went through my mind. I needed to write lists and find telephone numbers before Steve's name was released on the news.

This was a national air disaster and I had no idea what was about to occur in my life. I had no clue this accident was going to be as huge as it was.

There were certain people that I felt I should call personally; my boss, Steve's boss, and Steve's best friend Jimmy. It was exhausting. I couldn't do it anymore. I tried to sound strong on the telephone, but I was in shock. I was going through the motions and acting and reacting like I thought I should. But I had no idea what I said or how I really sounded.

I was concerned about how this would affect Steve's boss. The sudden loss of a valuable employee, who obviously worked hard, could not be easy. My husband traveled constantly. It was one of the downsides to his job. I wondered who would handle all of the unfinished projects now. Steve wouldn't be around to even bring them up to date. I wondered if these heads of corporations ever really thought about the families when they demanded that these men fly all over creation.

"It's my job, Joanne." Steve would say. But I knew he hated all of the traveling. He always commented that sometimes it was a waste of a lot of company money.

Within two days after the accident, his boss was sitting on the loveseat in our family room. He had the unpleasant duty to visit the new young widow and her now fatherless children. His job was to assure us that we would be well taken care of because my husband and their father made certain that if he died in an accident related to work, we would have plenty of insurance to get us by for a few years.

I tried to make this man feel comfortable. I watched him squirm as he sat alone on the loveseat trying to look at my children and me while we sat together across from him. He was obviously totally distraught himself. Not only did he lose his right hand man, and not only did he need to pick up all of the pieces at work, he had to look at me and my children in our eyes, knowing that my husband died because he was on a business trip for the company. Perhaps this business trip wasn't really all that necessary. Many times I would ask Steve if it were necessary for him to go out of town. Sometimes he would shrug his shoulders and admit that he could have handled the problem over the phone. I wondered if this was one of those times. Did I even want to know?

So I sat across from my husband's boss who was trying to assure me that Steve loved us very much. I already knew that. He was fumbling with a yellow piece of paper that he had written numbers on before he came to our home. This was the insurance. This was what I guess he thought would ease my mind and make me feel better. How trite. Didn't he know that nothing would make me feel better except my husband walking through the front door? At that moment in time I didn't give a thought about money or how we were going to survive financially. I was concerned about surviving emotionally. But this man was doing his job. He didn't have to be the one to come there and face us. He could have sent anyone. But he chose to come himself. I respected him for that.

He read to us the figures and explained about each insurance policy. Once again he repeated that Steve loved us very much and wanted to make sure if something happened to him, we would be well taken care of.

"Accidental death and dismemberment"...I lost it then. I knew if I would sit there and listen to these terms I would cry. So I shut him out. I didn't want to hear about accidental death and dismemberment. I couldn't listen at that moment. I looked at the color of his socks, rolled my eyes over his shoes, up to his shirt, and focused on the yellow piece of paper that was shaking in his hand. My ears focused on the light chatter from the helpful people in the kitchen handling all of the donated jello salads and meat trays.

He was obviously not comfortable in this position. While he spoke I thought about how blessed he was that in a few minutes he would be able to leave this sad house full of shocked and grieving people and go home to his wife. His normal life. It could have been my husband in his living room extending condolences to his wife. I wondered if that thought had ever crossed this man's mind. Then, I felt sorry for him. He looked lost. He looked responsible. I certainly didn't hold him responsible for my husband's death. It was an *accident*. The whole thing was just a stupid unexplainable *accident*.

Then he caught my attention again as he turned to my eighteen year old daughter and said something to her that would certainly impress her enough to change her life. He said, "Lisa, more than anything, your dad wanted you to finish college. We would talk about this all of the time. One of the most important dreams of your dad was for his children to go to college."

She smiled and nodded her head, eyes filling with tears. I smiled too, because I knew it was true. I do not even realize if this man knew the importance of what he just told both of my children. It was at that instant that my daughter decided that she would go back to college and graduate…in memory of her dad. I will always be grateful for my husband's boss for those few wise words. He was a brave man to enter our home in the middle of all of this chaotic painful uncertainty. I knew then, it wasn't easy.

MY FIFTEEN MINUTES...*plus*

◆

As soon as a list of victim's names was released to the public, I became bombarded with telephone calls from news stations, newspapers, magazines and Federal Express truckloads full of letters and videotapes from unethical leaching lawyers.

Every waking moment of television in the city of Pittsburgh was devoted to the USAir flight 427-airplane crash. It was constant. As soon as a list of names was released to the public, I became bombarded with telephone calls from news stations, newspapers, magazines and Federal Express truckloads full of letters and videotapes from unethical leaching lawyers. At the time, I didn't realize how widespread this airplane crash was. I only knew that my life as I had known it for twenty years was now interrupted and never going to be the same. I was in my own little depressed world. I had no clue that the entire city of Pittsburgh as well as the entire nation was also affected and grieving right along with us.

I agreed to do a short television interview with our local news in Pittsburgh. I don't know why I agreed. I was still in shock. The last thing I needed to worry about was going in front of a camera and talking. But I did it for Steve. I wanted everyone to know that he was a wonderful, loving human being that died, not just a name that ran across the television screen at the end of the newscast about the plane crash.

Another reason I agreed to be interviewed was because I had hoped that other family members would watch and try to get in touch with me. I wanted more than anything to talk with them. I needed to know if they were feeling the same shock as me. No one informed me that CNN would be picking up my little local news segment and soon all of the national television news shows would be knocking at my door and calling me on the telephone.

It is similar to when you are on a beach and you are holding this one piece of bread. You see one little lonely seagull flying around searching for food. You see nothing wrong with tossing a small piece of bread into the air for him to eat. Then suddenly, there are five more seagulls swarming down at you wanting their share of the bread. Then twenty. Before you know it, above you are hundreds of seagulls rapidly flying over your head for their split of that one piece of bread. You begin to start breaking the bread into smaller pieces throwing them up higher in the air and then further away from you so they will leave you alone. Then pretty soon the bread is gone. You have nothing else to give them. You scream, "GO AWAY!"

That was me with the media.

The inside of my house was filling up with relatives and friends, too many chocolate cakes and meat and cheese trays. There was too much havoc. Part of me wanted everyone to go home and leave my children and me alone so I could go into my bedroom, close the door, and cry quietly in peace. But the other part of me was grateful I had so many wonderful friends and family who stayed around me keeping me busy and my mind occupied. I didn't really want to be alone and think because it was too painful.

The newspapers were asking for photos of the victims. They sent one of their newspaper photographers to my home to photograph a picture of my husband that I had chosen. A young gentleman, probably in his late twenties or early thirties stood outside of my front door, not wanting to intrude. As I handed him the picture of Steve that I carefully picked from the most recent photo album, he asked me if I was related to the victim.

I stepped outside with him and proudly told him I was "the wife." I saw the color drain from his face and watched as his trembling hands carefully removed the photo from my hand. From the uneasy look upon his face as he extended his sympathy, I could sense he did not choose to be here. I tried to make small talk with him as he focused his camera onto my picture that was now laying on the hard cement step. I remember asking if he had any trouble finding my house. A silly question I realized later.

He looked down onto my street, pointed and nervously laughed and said, "No, not really, I just followed the cars!" I glanced down into the street and saw at least twenty cars parked on both sides of my street and up into my driveway which could easily hold six cars. I lived on a dead end street and there were usually no cars parked on it. It was quite an unusual site for me. It looked like one of those scenes where you think there is a big fun party going on. But this wasn't fun. And it wasn't a party.

This photographer's sense of sympathy for me and my family genuinely touched me. I understood this was just his job. I wanted my husband's picture in the newspaper along with all of the other victims. I told this photographer what a wonderful man my husband was and how much I was going to miss him. I told him I was so afraid the newspaper would find an awful picture of him from his file at work. My husband was too handsome, I had said. I wanted to choose the picture that would portray him correctly. He looked at me with such empathy; it was making me feel uncomfortable. I didn't want attention. I just wanted my normal life back again.

When the photographer was finished he quietly thanked me for taking the time to personally come outside with the picture and wanted me to know that the entire city was mourning this huge loss right along with us. He wished me well and sadly walked away. He probably got into his car and drove away with a heavy heart. And hopefully…glad to be alive.

I received telephone calls from every major network. I agreed to do *Dateline* and *CBS Morning News*. For Dateline, my backyard was transformed into a television studio complete with camera's, tripods with lighting foils and workers trying respectfully not to make eye contact with the widow. Most of the news people were very kind and respectful. They would ask us our permission to set up any sort of equipment or to enter a room. They expressed their sympathy before the cameras rolled and made sure I was comfortable in answering their questions.

I remember sitting across from Chris Hanson of "Dateline" talking about Steve. I told him how sweet and intelligent my husband was and how all he wanted to do was come home to his family. After I told him what a wonderful marriage we had and how much we loved each other, he asked me what this plane crash had taken from me. I looked at him straight in the eyes and at that very moment in time, I meant it with my whole heart. I answered the question in a very serious sad voice that wasn't even recognizable to me. I said, "My life…my whole life…and my happiness…I don't think I will ever be happy again." I looked into his face and shook my head from side to side saying "nah." Tears ready to fall. I truly believed my life was over.

Monday morning, live on "CBS Morning News"…via satellite. We had to awaken before dawn, dress and make-up. The news crew entered our home while it was still pitch black outside. Parked in front of my house was a huge truck with a large satellite dish pointed to the stars. It wasn't difficult for me to be awake that early. I did not sleep at night anyway. My sister and her husband were there with us.

When I watch that particular segment now, I can't believe I did it. My voice is deep and slow and I looked and sounded as though I hadn't slept in days. I *hadn't* slept in days. I announced that I would like to see USAir purchase the crash site land and turn it into a memorial for all of the 427 families to visit. One hundred and thirty-two people died in that area. The land should never be used for anything. I knew then, that part of my husband would always be there. I looked tired. I looked like I was still in shock. I was…on both accounts.

THE AIRLINES

◆

*I yelled at my USAir "family coordinator," "**You bring me his car but you can't bring me his body! You go back and you tell your people that he wasn't just a statistic. He wasn't just a number. He was my husband. He was their father!**" She didn't know what to say or what to do. She walked towards her own car and sat down inside it, constantly writing little notes inside her notebook. I thought to myself, "Go ahead and report this to your company as a widow gone mad."*

I was assigned four different airline coordinators who unfortunately had the dreadful task of representing the airline that just crashed killing my husband. Needless to say, I was not too happy with anyone representing USAir at that moment in time. I wanted answers that they could not give. I wanted to know where my husband's body was and why the plane crashed. I realize now that the people I was in contact with did not know the answers. This was an airline disaster that no one was qualified or prepared to handle, especially emotional support for the family members.

My first airline co-coordinator told me that she was not trained in bereavement; her job was working in sales. They pulled her out of her department and sent her to Pittsburgh to deal with the families. I needed to know what I was supposed to do about holding a funeral without a body and she was concerned the day I chose might conflict with a wedding she had to attend. It was not her fault. She wasn't properly trained.

Many months later I would become one of several family members who would be interviewed by the Red Cross to help implement a program for the families of disasters. It would be known as "The Family Assistance Act." I needed to recall all of my personal unpleasant incidences that I had experienced with the airlines and the media after the airplane crash. I made suggestions on how I thought things could have been handled in a tragic and unexpected situation. The first one being the notification of the families in a timely manner. I think the waiting and the "not knowing" was one of the hardest things we had to endure. Especially hearing from one airline representative that my husband was a "no show" on that flight leading some of us to think he was still alive. That false hope was just inexcusably cruel. I also needed emotional support from someone who was experienced in bereavement and separate from the airline company.

I am proud to say that in October of 1996, along with other family members of various airplane crashes, I stood behind President Clinton and witnessed him signing the "The Family Assistance Act." This would support more compassionate treatment of families in the aftermath of air tragedies. This would also insure that families receive more timely information about the progress of the investigation, immediate emotional support and privacy. It was a start. Now when there is a national disaster and I hear how the Red Cross has sent trained people to help with the survivors and family members, I secretly smile because I was one of the people who helped make that happen.

After my first television interview, my wish came true. Another widow from the 427 plane crash called me on the telephone. Her name was Jane and she would be my first contact. She gave me her telephone number and we called each other a few times and talked that first month. We discussed how our children were reacting. I had such a desire to meet with the other family members of the plane crash. But that would come several weeks later with the help of the Allegheny County Health Department.

Days after the crash, I still did not have my husband's body or any information stating that there was positive proof that he was on that airplane. Not knowing the severity of the crash, I was still hoping that somehow he was thrown from the plane, crawled to safety and blacked out. Any moment he would awaken, hitch a ride from a stranger and come home.

My house was still constantly full of family and friends. My sister Donna was in charge of everything including screening all of my phone calls. I was still receiving invitations to appear on various television programs, radio talk shows and magazine and newspaper reporters were calling for interviews. Several of my friends, were in charge of keeping lists of who brought what food so I could properly send thank you notes and they made sure everyone was fed.

I was exhausted from lack of sleep. My cousin Carol suggested she sit with me alone in my bedroom and that I try to rest. She held my hand as I tried to close my eyes. Suddenly, I heard my husband talking below us. I jumped up, ran down the stairs into the family room and saw that it was his brother talking. The disappointed look on my face changed into terror as I sobbed in his arms. He sounded so much like Steve. I wanted my husband back.

The airlines kept in touch with us via the telephone. Each time I received a new coordinator they would ask me the same questions over and over again. They wanted me to describe my husband by the color of his hair, eyes, height and weight. They asked me what he was wearing. Did he wear glasses or contact lenses? Did I remember the color of his tie, his socks, and his shoes? Did he have on a wedding ring, a watch? Were they engraved? I had to reach deep in my memory…

"Yes his ring was engraved with our initials and our wedding date!"

What was the color and the brand of his watch?

"It was a Seiko…gold."

Was it engraved?

I couldn't remember what I had engraved on it. My mind went blank. I had engraved two watches for him. One said, "You're the one I want to go through time with." The other watch read: "To the only man who makes me feel at HOME in this world." I couldn't think. I couldn't find his other watch either. Pressure, pressure, pressure. I wanted all of my husband's belongings returned to me. I didn't want them lying in some airplane hanger or coroner's office or crash site for looters to find.

Did he have any scars, any identifiable birthmarks?

"Yes he had a scar from an appendectomy. He had many scars from childhood horsing around with his brothers…" Was this really necessary to remember everything? Even though it pained me to keep describing him over and over again, I answered each time, like a dutiful child, with the hope that it would somehow expedite finding and identifying my husband. I wanted him home.

Months later after reading the reports of the plane crash's devastation and the coroners report of the victims remains, it infuriated me that the airlines would put me through so much pain and grief asking me those questions again and again when it really did not matter what color his eyes were or the color of his hair. I felt like a fool. The airlines, however, would state that they were trying to protect the families. They needed all of the information that they could gather. I suppose everyone was just doing what he or she was told.

I wanted my husband's car, which was still at the Pittsburgh airport. It was a red Saturn sports coupe that could not be towed and I did not want anyone inside driving it. The airlines agreed to locate it at the airport-parking garage and bring it to my home. I had to give them my keys to the car since Steve's keys were with him when the plane crashed. I watched from my bedroom window as his little red car perched on top of a flatbed tow truck was carried down my street. It was as though I was watching a red float in a parade. Very surrealistic. All of the neighbors were standing outside watching. I ran down the stairs and out to the front of my house and stared at my husband's car. This was so much a part of him. He was in this car everyday. Having it delivered back to me without him was like a horse returning without its cowboy. I walked along side of the car and lightly touched the doors, tears falling.

I knew everyone was watching me and I must have looked like I lost my mind. I yelled at my USAir "family coordinator," "You bring me his car but you can't bring me his body! You go back and you tell your people that he wasn't just a statistic. He wasn't just a number. He was my husband. He was their father!" (I pointed to my children) She didn't know what to say or what to do. She walked towards her own car and sat down inside it constantly writing little notes inside her notebook. I thought to myself, "Go ahead and report this to your company as a widow gone mad."

After they slowly slid the car onto the street, I sat inside the drivers seat and slowly slid my hands over the steering wheel trying to touch each inch of what he last touched. I picked up a cigarette butt from the ashtray and put it to my mouth. Ordinarily that would have disgusted me, but I needed to press it against my lips. I picked up his coffee mug and ran it along my mouth tasting the stale scent of coffee, knowing his lips touched it last. In the sun visor was the ticket for the airport parking garage with that ominous date Sept 8th stamped on it. A cassette tape of Forrest Gump music was in the tape deck. Tom Hanks reminded me of my husband; handsome, an eloquent speaker and a great sense of humor. We always made sure we watched his movies. Forrest Gump will forever remind me of the last movie we saw together.

Scattered in the console were some loose change and a candy bar wrapper. I smiled as I thought of him enjoying each bite of this candy bar and then I cried knowing it was probably his last taste of chocolate. I would save each of these things in a plastic zip-lock bag and look at them over and over again. It was something I needed to do. I loved him so much; I did not want to let any part of him go. I wanted him to know how much I loved him and that I always would.

THE FUNERAL

◆

Ten whole days passed by before we would schedule the most unusual funeral.

Under normal circumstances when a person dies, there is a funeral and a burial within a few days and people can come and pay their respects and give their condolences. There is a closure.

Because we had no body, we did not know what to do. So we did nothing. We waited each day for the county coroner to make as many positive identifications as efficiently and quickly as he could. But this type of tragedy was not anything they had ever experienced. It was difficult for everyone who was involved: the families, the hundreds of volunteers, the people who worked in the crash site, the airlines, and the entire city of Pittsburgh.

People were sending food and flowers and wanted to give us their sympathy. My telephone was constantly ringing. Someone was always screening my calls for me. We needed to make funeral arrangements without having a body to bury. Too many people wanted to express their sympathy to us. And I just couldn't handle any more people coming to my house. It was too exhausting.

Ten whole days passed by before we would schedule the most unusual funeral. The airlines instructed us to choose a casket. They suggested we have a closed casket with a picture of Steve on top of it. My husband was too full of life to have an empty casket be his last representation. So I decided to spread the word that we would have the casket open and if people wanted to bring something that reminded them of Steve, they could put it in the casket and we would bury it. My children and I chose his Pittsburgh Steelers sweatshirt and I placed a framed cross stitching that I had made for him of a father and two children that read, "Anyone can be a father, but it takes someone special to be a daddy."

Many of our friends and family placed letters, poems and cards inside the coffin. Children drew pictures, and brought small stuffed animals. My cousin and her husband brought a Steelers's football, my aunt placed one of her own pieces of art work, while others placed snapshots of them with Steve, beer bottles, video boxes from movies, packs of Marlboro cigarettes, a pizza box from former fellow employees, signifying where they all used to eat lunch together, humorous computer pictures and many more little treasures that reminded them of Steve.

One of my favorite items was a framed letter typed to Steve from a former co-worker, reminiscing about the time Steve was called into work in the middle of the night to help him fix a computer crisis. Steve immediately woke up, dressed and drove to work. He stopped and bought his friend a Big Mac and a coke, rolled up his sleeves and figured out the problem. The co-worker wrote that in a person's lifetime, we were suppose to be able to count the number of true friends on just one hand and that now all he had to do was find four more.

Seeing all of these precious thoughtful things brought warmth to my children and me. Steve was such a kind man and had such a wonderful sense of humor. Seeing that people took the time to pay tribute to him made us feel we did the right thing. So many people loved and cared about him. It helped us to see how he touched all of their lives too.

We had two exhausting days at the funeral home greeting guests who came to give us their sympathy. The lines never seemed to end. I remember trying so hard to be strong, but not wanting to go back after the first visitation. It was so depleting. But I did it for my family. I did it for Steve. I was still in such shock. I had no idea what I was saying to anyone. It was a complete act. I kept trying to be strong just to get through everything in one piece. I found myself comforting the visitors and trying to make them feel at ease with us. Each person that came in would start me crying all over again. It was probably the most emotionally exhausting thing I ever had to do in my life.

We had to have a memorial mass at our church and not a funeral mass because there was no body inside the casket. It was now almost two weeks after the plane crashed. With the help of one of our closest friends, Dan Keller, we had chosen which scriptures would be read, which songs would be sung, who would sing them, and who would speak about Steve. It was almost like putting on a show. Everything had to be choreographed. My own concern was getting through the memorial mass in one piece and not collapsing in front of everyone. I did not want to say good-bye to my husband because I still was not convinced he was on that plane.

The immediate family which consisted of my family and Steve's family met at the funeral home before the memorial mass. We would ride to the church together in two limousines. Moments before we left the funeral home, our airline coordinator called the funeral home to talk to my sister.

My sister came to me and said, "Joanne, the airline coordinator just called and we have good news."

I did not want to hear the news. I knew what she was going to say. On the news broadcast that morning they announced that the Coroner would be posting the first group of names of those they could identify by dental records. I felt I still needed to hang on to the tiny bit of hope that Steve was not on that airplane. I needed all of my strength to get through this memorial/funeral mass. I did not want to know if they identified my husband's remains. I did not want to hear it.

I looked at my sister, gritted my teeth and I said, "Donna, don't say it. The only "GOOD" news that you could possibly tell me is that they found Steve and he is alive and he will be here in fifteen minutes." I didn't care if he walked in, was guided inside in a wheelchair, or pushed in on a gurney. She looked at me like a mother would look at a child and did what she thought needed to be done despite my request.

She blurted it out. "They found his wedding ring."

I was livid. I walked into the room where the casket laid open still full of all of the memento's and I angrily shuffled things around inside it. What I wanted to do was throw them against the wall. I wasn't mad at my sister for telling me the news. I was mad that now I had to attend this memorial mass knowing it was really going to be final. Now I had to go to church and face a crowd of people knowing that my husband really was dead.

As I walked down the aisle of our church with my daughter on my left side and my son on the right, I could see the entire church filled with people, tissues raised to their noses and eyes. I recalled another time when I walked down that very church aisle with everybody's eyes on me. It was over twenty years ago in June; on the day I married Steve. Here I was with a full church watching me again, only this time it was for his funeral.

Now that I had the information about finding his wedding ring, there was a good possibility he really was on that plane. Knowing that he was probably dead allowed me to listen to the eulogies with a sense of appreciation. All of the tributes were written with such love and admiration.

Our priest, Father Franco, told everyone how he used to watch Steve and me as we sat in the same section of the church every week during mass. Father Franco and I were on the board of director's for a senior citizen's high-rise together and he would always tease Steve about my strong opinions on how things should be done and Steve would just laugh and wish him luck! It made me smile.

Dan Keller, spoke about their close and wonderful friendship and Steve's sense of commitment for our community and his loyalty and his love for his family. Another good friend, Paul Brown read a letter written by my brother honoring Steve. Steve's cousin Paul spoke about him as a young boy and the closeness they shared growing up with such a loving family. His brother David, who was probably the closest person to Steve besides the kids and me, broke down several times before finishing his heartfelt tribute. And Steve's boss spoke kindly about Steve as a loyal dedicated worker.

When everyone was finished, my daughter read a poem that she wrote a few days earlier about being "Daddy's Little Girl", and I even spoke about our love for each other. There were so many tissues being used that morning, there was not a dry eye in the house.

He was covered in every aspect of his life: Husband, Father, Brother, Friend, Cousin, and Worker. Steve would have been so touched to be honored this way.

"All of this, just for me?" He would have asked, feeling incredibly humble.

After the funeral, I was now ready to start the grieving process.

A TIME TO GRIEVE

◆

Grieving consumes almost every moment of every day. It turns into an octopus as it wraps itself around our mind, our body, and our heart and strangles our every breath.

Everyone warns us not to take our loved ones for granted. Of course that is never our intention, but at some point, we become comfortable and the worrying ceases, then just when we think everything is perfect…just when we think it is all right to relax…bang! Our entire world comes crumbling down. Every dream, every plan, and every thought become "used to's" and "remember when's." Grieving consumes almost every moment of every day. It turns into an octopus as it wraps itself around our mind, our body, and our heart and strangles our every breath. At least for the first six months to a year. Some experience the strangle longer, some shorter. But we all share the experience at some point after the death of a loved one.

You need to learn so much when you lose a spouse. You have to deal with things that used to be his/her job. You can eventually learn how to balance the checkbook, change a furnace filter, and even learn about blue-chip stocks. Someone can teach you the difference between a screwdriver and a wrench, and someone can show you the correct way to open and close a can of paint. If you are a widower, someone can tell you to separate the colors from the whites in the laundry room and someone can teach you how to cook.

But what no one can teach you, what no one can simply show you, is how to alleviate the pain. That comes only with the proverbial span called "time." And I am here to tell you that it really does occur.

Time is a mender. Not drugs, not alcohol, not even the company of other human beings will heal the pain. They may put the inevitable on a temporary hold, but sooner or later you must deal with the loss. You must learn how to rehabilitate all over again and go forward with life. For if you truly loved this person, what better way to respect their memory than to show them that because of their love, their strength will carry you through. And although right now you may not agree, life is a good thing. It is worth going on in this world. There may be times when living without your loved one is out of the question. There will be many bad days ahead but there will also be a few good days thrown in there to just confuse you. Eventually the good days will begin to out number the bad. And you will notice it.

You will learn to take advantage of the good days, before the grief attacks you again. You will make telephone calls to people you have been putting off. You will perform functions like paying your bills or sorting through mail and other things you may be incapable of doing once the depression hits. And you will learn not to be fooled because the depression and the emptiness can and will return with the flip of a switch. It can be a piece of a memory; a song on the radio, or a line from a movie that can trigger it all over again and suddenly the smile upon your face is now replaced with tears.

Get used to it. But be assured it is only temporary. For someday, the good days will out number the bad, you will be able to breathe again without sighing so deeply. You will be able to laugh again without feeling guilty. And those special memories that now make you tear up and cry, will become a part of your past. Those memories will form a small smile upon your face.

Time does help but remember one thing: although time is a mender, it never really heals completely. You will carry this scar with you for the rest of your life. In the middle of a joyous, happy, fun occasion, it may appear out of nowhere…somehow, something will remind you. You will always think about your loved one. And that is all right. You don't want to forget them and you shouldn't. As time goes on, the pain of thinking of them will just hurt less.

NOW WHAT?

◆

I was scared. I was petrified. The pain was too unbearable. All I wanted to do was cry and sleep.

The day after the funeral, when all of your friends and relatives go back to their own normal lives and the vases of beautiful flowers that were delivered to your house begin to wilt and the baskets of oranges and apples begin breeding fruit flies, and you find yourself sitting in the house for the first time, completely alone, and the only sound you hear is the refrigerator humming, and panic slaps you in the face, the one question that echoes loudly is "Now what?"

It had been over two weeks and my loving family made certain that I was never left alone. Finally after the funeral I insisted that my daughter and her boyfriend go out. I assured them I would be fine. But I really wasn't prepared for the first time I was alone in my own home.

The funeral director presented me with a small plaid zippered case filled with extra holy cards engraved with my husband's name and death date, several boxes of thank you notes, and all of the Mass cards and envelopes with donations. As I flipped through the papers, I searched for instructions as to what I was suppose to do now. How in the world could I ever get through this without the man I loved with all of my heart? How in the world could I possibly ever get through the night much less a week, a month, and a year, or my whole life? It was just too much to ask. We were partners in this relationship. I was not supposed to be going through life alone. I was scared. I was petrified. The pain was too unbearable. All I wanted to do was cry and sleep.

If I slept, there might be a chance that I would dream of him. Sometimes the dreams felt so realistic, that I actually felt I had been with him all through the night. But then I would awaken to an empty bed and he was not there beside me. I felt worse. There were times that I would wake up in the morning and not open my eyes for just a few seconds. I would wonder if the plane crash was a big bad dream and lying beside me was my husband comfortably sleeping. I would even welcome the unpleasant sound of his snoring. I silently whispered a little prayer to God to please let the plane crash be one big nightmare. Then slowly I slid my left leg onto his side of the bed hoping to feel some part of him. Slowly it would glide over and it would find nothing. I would lay motionless, enveloped by the stillness, the emptiness. Trapped inside this nightmare of a tragedy unable to escape. Sometimes I would cry, sometimes sigh, and sometimes I would not even want to get out of bed. Another day of grieving.

I had to resign from my job because I couldn't concentrate anymore. I was a buyer for a card and gift store and I loved my job. I tried to go back to work several times, but I was useless. All I did was cry. I had no desire to shop any longer. I needed time to get my emotional strength back. My boss was wonderful and told me the door would always be open for my return whenever I felt I was able.

Although the temporary diversions consisting of chatty visits, lunches and phone calls from my friends did occupy my mind, I continually found myself alone with my thoughts at night and on weekends. Weekends are time for families. Husbands are usually home mowing the lawns, working in the yard, washing the car, and doing family activities. The kids are usually running in and out of the house and so many things are going on. Most of my friends had husbands. So I would not hear from them until Monday. Weekends were the worst for me. That was the time when Steve and I would go camping or shopping or go for long rides. We would visit flea markets, go to afternoon matinee movies or just lay around the house doing nothing. But we did nothing together. We used to live for weekends. This was our R&R time together. We worked hard all week for the weekend. Now weekends were the loneliest. Weekends were the pits. I hated weekends with a passion now. Sometimes I would lie in my bed and watch TV and I would have to close my window. The sound of the lawn mower running from my next-door neighbor's yard would make me think of Steve and the bitterness would arrive like a burning sour stomach.

Losing contact with the outside world would have been a major mistake. But I hated being around other couples, other families and anyone who was remotely happy. It is not that I am a jealous person, quite the opposite. I could no longer endure the pain of not having my own happiness anymore. No matter how many people were in the room, I felt totally alone. I believed I did not belong anywhere.

I not only felt the pain for me, but the pain for my children as well. I always prided myself with being a strong protective mother. Now I felt stripped of my parental duty to protect my children from unhappiness, to protect them from harm. For the first time in my life, I felt like I was not doing a good job and there wasn't anything I could do about it. I had no strength. I had no desire. Watching my children see me in this state of mind bothered me more than they will ever know. I could not bake them cookies anymore. I could barely cook dinner. I did not even want to clean. Our home once decorated with a joyful family consistency was no longer a happy place to be. The former homeroom mother, PTA President, softball coach, and Mother of the Year, had lost all of her passion and she just didn't want to live anymore.

THE WILL TO LIVE

◆

"Here is the test to find whether your mission on earth is finished: If you're alive, it isn't."

I will be totally honest about this subject. I would be lying if I said that it never occurred to me not to go on with my life. It did. Twice.

The first time was two months after my husband died. The pain was so heavy, so severe; nothing, and no one could help. I was driving home alone after having dinner with a group of my female cousins. It was the first time we were all together since the funeral and everyone was sweet, and sympathetic. I sensed the sad looks of empathy while everyone tried desperately to act normal around me. But I knew the minute I would leave for the lady's room, the whispers of "How is she really doing?" circulated as fast as bees around a hive. Everyone was still very concerned about me.

In the car through the dark on the drive home, I thought about how they would be going home to their husbands and to their normal lives. I would probably be going home to an empty dark house because I was certain that my teenagers would be out. I dreaded going back to the house of gloom. There is nothing worse than going home to an empty house. No one to welcome you home and ask how your evening went.

No one to sip coffee or tea with. No one. The emptiness began to strangle its way around my heart once again.

As I was lost in my thoughts, I began driving over a long bridge. I entertained the thought of steering very quickly to the right and flying over the bridge ending my pain. I am ashamed to admit it now but thoughts of no one stopped me. At that moment, I did not think of the ramifications my death would have been on my children or my family or my friends. I could not think of anything but alleviating the pain. I did not want to feel it anymore. I missed my husband too much and did not want to go on without him. However, something triggered my brain for one split second and made me remember that I had not yet put my will in order. I did not want my children to have to worry about all of the problems of settling an estate without a will. I made a deal with myself. I would go home, put my things in order and then when I was completely ready, I would drive back to the bridge and do it. The deal allowed me to complete the drive over the bridge.

A few minutes later on the road to my house reality set in. In a matter of a few seconds, I could have been dead. My life would have been over. I pulled off to the side of the road and took a deep breath. What in the world could I have been thinking? Within five minutes I was glad I was still alive. After I arrived home and pulled into the garage, both of my teenagers were there. They greeted me with hugs and warm conversation.

That night, I reflected on my close encounter with death. I was about as close to suicide as one gets without actually doing it. I used to think that those who committed suicide were self-centered uncaring people taking the easy way out! Now I believe that whatever it is that makes a person follow through with ending his life must have been so terribly painful. All they wanted to do was to get rid of the pain. Now when I hear of a suicide, I silently say a prayer of peace for their soul. I hope that when someone feels the necessity to end his life, he reconsiders. Chances are that within five minutes he will be glad he waited.

The second time I thought about ending my life was a whole year later. You would think that after a whole year the pain would have been gone. Not quite. With the anniversary of the plane crash front-page news again all over Pittsburgh and the media asking me for interviews and statements, I had anxiety again. There were memorial services to attend and speeches to give. After all the events, I once again found myself with the question…"Okay…now what?" I lived through a whole year. I held down the fort. I paid the bills, changed all the burned out light bulbs, even the ones I could never reach. I learned the difference between an IRA and the IRS. Whatever I could not physically do myself, I paid people to do it for me. I hired a financial advisor, an accountant, and a wallpaper hanger who also painted. I found a man who trimmed trees and hedges. I've been trying to keep everything going. So, when is Steve coming back? I wanted to show him how I was now driving on the highway. I wanted him to see that I kept the house in good shape. I wanted him to see what a good job I had done. I needed my pat on the back.

Guess what? The pat was never going to come. Not from him anyway. The second year the realization set in and I had to admit that he really was not coming home. This was not a temporary separation or an extended business trip. This was it. That pain started to attack me again. That shield of denial no longer protected me. My husband was gone forever. I was on my own. We became me.

The date was September 29, 1995. It was the birthday of my father who had died nineteen years before. I found myself walking around a lake near my house. I had started a walking program months before to exercise my mind and body. I had already written in my journal twice that day. I knew I was having a bad time if I wrote twice in one day. I began to think about Steve. I truly did not know if I could do another whole year again without him. It was too difficult. It was too lonely. I was too tired. It hurt knowing that I would have to endure yet another holiday season, another anniversary, another birthday. The lake began to look very appealing to me. I stood on a concrete pier for twenty minutes gazing into the water. Once again I only thought about relieving the pain. I wanted it to end. I prayed to God, I prayed to the angels, I prayed to Steve for help.

This was not a ploy for sympathy or attention because no one knew but me. I did not want any more sympathy or attention. I just wanted to be normal again. Standing at the edge of the concrete pier, I wondered just how deep this part of the lake was. What if I didn't drown? What if I jumped in, changed my mind, and swam to shore? Then I would be soaking drenching wet and all of the runners jogging by would wonder why I looked like a drowned rat. I would have to walk at least twenty minutes back to my car, soaking wet. I canceled the lake date and went home. Later that evening still feeling depressed, I turned on the television. I watched a program that would change my life forever and hopefully suicide will never again enter my mind.

The program was "20/20" with Barbara Walters interviewing Christopher Reeve. I sat on the floor of my room with a box of tissues in one hand and wept. Here was this remarkable man in a wheelchair unable to even breathe on his own and I was ready to throw away a perfectly good functional body. His sweet smile shined through to my soul. He inspired me to want to live. I wrote in my journal for the third time that day. If Steve would have survived that plane crash and needed to be in a wheel chair, I definitely would have stood by him. Just like Christopher Reeve's wife stated, "In Sickness and in Health." I was in love with his mind, his heart, and his soul. I sobbed and felt incredibly guilty for thinking about suicide. I could breathe. I could walk. I could run. I had the capabilities to do so much. I could help others as he helped me. I vowed that night to live my life to the fullest, whatever that might be. No more self pity. No more thoughts of jumping into lakes or driving over bridges. I now wanted to live.

For Christmas that year, my sister bought me a box of little "angel cards." One of the cards touched my heart and I still carry it around with me in my wallet.

It reads, "Here is the test to find whether your mission on earth is finished: If you're alive, it isn't."

I purchased a picture of Christopher Reeve in his Superman attire, right arm extended, his powerful fist pointing towards the sky. Although the large red "S" on the front of his costume is for "Superman," to me, the "S" stands for "Steve." I have the picture hanging in my office as a reminder of how fragile we are, yet how strong we can be. Whenever I do not feel like getting out of bed or walking, or working, I think of Christopher Reeve and the strength he gave me on September 29, 1995, and I move. I see that full smile of his and that twinkle in those beautiful blue eyes and I become inspired all over again. Someday I would like to thank him for saving my life.

HIS THINGS

◆

I remember washing a load of laundry a few days after he died and I saw his clothes in the wash, not knowing if I should wash them or throw them away.

When do we remove their clothes and what do we do with them?

This is a personal decision. Everybody has the right to wait until they are ready.

I left the very last bath towel my husband used, hanging on the shower door for a full year. I never did wash it. Some days I would hold it close to me knowing he dried himself with it that last morning. I would try and smell the scent of his soap.

I remember washing a load of laundry a few days after he died and I saw his clothes in the wash, not knowing if I should wash them or throw them away. I just looked down at them with such sadness knowing he would never wear them again. I decided to wash his clothes and placed them in his dresser drawers as if he were still alive. That was the first of one of the hardest things I had to do.

Some nights I would sleep with his sweatshirt on, feeling his embrace. I would wear his shirts knowing they were last on his body. There were nights, lonely nights, that I would take out of the closet one of his suit jackets, hold it tightly up against me and close my eyes while

I slow danced to a beautiful song on the radio all by myself in our bedroom. Our love was so strong, if there was such a thing as the hereafter, I wanted him to know I was missing him. I wanted him to know how I still loved him with all of my heart.

I can make some suggestions and also tell you what worked for me. But then again, I had 93-year-old grandmother who for seventeen years forbid anyone to touch my grandfather's clothes after he passed away. They hung in the closet right next to hers until she died. I always thought that was a little extreme. But we respected her wishes.

I was a little more practical than Grandma. I needed more closet space! I kept creeping over onto his side of the closet squashing all of his suits. Finally, one day I decided I would make three piles. One pile I would keep for sentimental reasons, the second would be given to his brothers and the third to charity. After about three hours of gently folding and caressing each item, I noticed that my "keep" pile was way too large. I went through his clothes again, this time being more selective. I brought my children into my room and allowed them to be a part of this. Anything they wanted they were more than welcomed to take. My son asked for his father's leather jacket, my daughter took a favorite Nike sweatshirt that her dad always wore. I told myself that I was not giving them all away; I was just moving them to the attic. That way I did not feel like I was getting rid of him. I fully knew that someday down the road, I would be able to bid them adieu, but for right now, this was the deal. (I made many deals with myself!)

Left hanging on the lower left side of the closet was two of his suit jackets and two favorite sweatshirts from his colleges. Every once in a while when I was in a weepy mood, I would sit on the floor with a box of tissues and hug the clothes. I would hold them tightly to my chest, trying desperately to be in touch with him.

His bathroom items, the shaver, hairbrush, comb, deodorant, cologne, etc., I packed inside of his travel case and placed it neatly on the top shelf in the bathroom closet. I knew that someday I would find it silly to keep such things and throw them away. Still standing tall beside my toothbrush stood his. I did not know what to do with it. Eventually I took it out of the holder. Seeing my toothbrush every morning standing alone was some sort of symbolism of how I felt in this world. There is something special about seeing two toothbrushes together in a holder.

The night after the memorial mass, the funeral director brought to our home a large white leather zippered bag. Typed neatly on a sticker glued to the bag was simply, "Stephen M. Shortley." Inside were all of the contents found at the crash site that belonged to my husband.

Thirty-seven years of life, a wife, two children, a mortgage and years of college and hard work, all compacted into this one 16 by 20 white leather bag. This was what was left of a man who worked so hard for his family. This was what remained of someone who happened to be at the wrong place at the wrong time.

I sat on the floor in the formal living room holding the bag. Around me were my children, my sister and the funeral director. I carefully unzipped it and spilled out the contents onto the white carpet. Everything smelled like jet fuel. On the floor laid his black leather *pocket day-timer*, the corners of the pages folded down to that ominous date, "September 8th 1994." Written in the memo were several airline names, flight numbers and times. USAir's flight 427 was among them. That was the flight that should have gotten him home the earliest. That was the one he unfortunately took.

Also laying on the floor was his wallet, which was now empty. All of the contents of his wallet...his credit cards, library card, AAA card, drivers license, pictures of me and our children would all be in a smaller see-through plastic bag. These items would be known as "The Personal Effects."

I shuffled through the pile of papers that contained his name, his notebooks and portfolio's, all in perfect shape, and found what I was looking for the most. It was in a tiny plastic bag. I picked it up and saw the small gold figure of what used to be my husband's wedding ring. I pulled it out of the bag and gasped in horror. It was no longer round. It was oval.

Something made it oval and that horrified me. I wondered if his finger was crushed. Did someone step on it at the crash site? There were so many unanswered questions. I checked the inside of the ring and read the inscription..."JP to SMS 6-14-74" and was assured it was Steve's. The next day I would go to the mall, have it cleaned, purchase a gold chain and wear it around my neck. I decided to leave it oval for a while because that was how it was found. His ring would become a part of me now. That would be my small little tribute to him for the rest of my life.

His watch was still missing, as was his brief case and laptop computer. In a few months I would have the opportunity to go to a USAir site and walk around a long table and view all of the other unclaimed "Personal Effects" and search for something that might have belonged to my husband. I would go there and look at things that used to belong to other living people. I felt like I was intruding on people's personal belongings. It was so dreamlike. Laying on this table were paperback books, (that these people never finished reading) some torn, some in great shape, some charred from the fire. A tattered bible, broken rosary beads, unidentified wallet sized pictures of children and families with smiles, many pieces of jewelry from wedding rings to broken necklaces. Belt Buckles, (I wondered where the rest of the belt had gone), purses, wallets, and many other articles.

I picked up several wristwatches. Some of the watches displayed the time of the crash, which was an eerie sight. They stopped immediately upon impact. And yet there were a few watches that were still ticking. Had it not been so terribly emotional at that moment, I would have joked to the person I was with, suggesting that this would have made a hell of a commercial for the watch company. "Takes a licking and keeps on ticking!" But I had no sense of humor anymore. I said nothing.

My suggestion when it comes to "The things," is to be reasonable and do what makes you comfortable. Take your time. Don't allow any well-meaning family members or friends to rush you into getting rid of anything until you are ready. Sooner or later you will determine when the time is right.

SURVIVAL

◆

I had to remember this was a whole new ball game now. I was the pitcher, the catcher, and the first man on base. I needed to be in control when I was up at bat.

Also included in that little suitcase given by the funeral director should have been a list of survival needs.

Being alone in the house with or without children, all of the responsibility was now mine. One of my biggest fears was being alone in the dark during a power outage. I needed to prepare myself. I went to the store and purchased several flashlights and several packages of batteries. I placed the flashlights in places where I could locate them in the dark. Making sure I did not place all of them in the bottom kitchen drawer, I put one on the corner of my nightstand next to my bed, one in the living room on the bottom left side of my coffee table and one in the basement on the shelf above my washing machine.

I utilized all of those candles we used to use for romantic evenings. Now they had a different purpose. I kept the candles out where I could find them with matches right next to them. (Be careful if you have small children) In the first two years, I used the flashlights and candles at least four times during power outages and lightening storms.

Before anything happened, I acquired, names and phone numbers from family and friends of a trustworthy plumber, an electrician, a reputable furnace man, a landscaper, a snowplower and I tried to find an honest handyman. I learned that I could not and did not always want to depend on friends and family members. They have their own households to take care of. I hated being a burden to anyone. Besides, you will find that after a certain time, all the free offers of help dwindle down.

I also had to learn where the main water valve was. My water heater broke unexpectedly in the middle of the night. Water heaters do that for no special reason and without warning. When water heaters break, they don't just stop heating water, they sometimes crack and water gushes all over the floor. I needed to shut off the water. I didn't even know there *was* a main valve let alone where to find it. I also needed to locate the circuit breaker box and learn how to set the circuit breaker off.

I bought plenty of boxes of tissue. I kept one in every room of the house, and placed a box inside of my car. I bought a back scratcher to assist me for those times when no one was around and I had an itch right in the middle of my back. I bought a jar opener to help me open those tightly sealed jars that only men seem to have the strength to open.

I always had my car filled with gas, in case of an emergency. I bought a cellular phone and took it with me everywhere I went. I needed to have some time away from my children and having the phone by my side certainly gave me peace of mind. It also eased my mind in case I got stranded on the road, I could phone for help. I had to remember this was a whole new ball game now. I was the pitcher, the catcher, and the man on first base. I needed to be prepared *before* things happened. I tried to make it easier on myself whenever I could because now, there was no husband to come to my rescue anymore. I no longer had my hero. I was it!

I needed to learn about finances. I did not surrender my personal business totally to anyone. Although I hired a financial advisor that I trusted, I tried to understand what was occurring financially at all times. This was my children's money and mine. The only person I could truly trust was no longer here…it was now up to me. This was difficult because Steve always handled the finances in our family. I was afraid I was going to make a mistake. I would balance the checkbook to the penny and hold my breath each month.

Even if you are financially independent, do not loan, sell or give anything away for at least one full year, unless you are absolutely certain you no longer need it. Everyone warned me to wait at least one year before I did anything major. I did not keep Steve's red car because every time I would come home and see it in the garage, I thought he was home and it hurt when I realized that he wasn't. Almost a year later I wished I had kept it.

The definition of insurance and settlement is not money won in a lottery. Money won in a lottery is a joyous occasion for celebration. The money that my children and I received was because the person we loved most in this world was no longer with us. That is no reason for celebration. The money we received is no way a compensation for the many painful sleepless nights, the nightmare of what he must have endured during those final seconds of his life, not to mention the agony and mental stress we will encounter for the remainder of our lives.

Those who really knew what kind of a loving family we were knew that no amount of money erased the void in our lives. I would have given anything to have my husband back. No amount of money can take the place of peace of mind.

Many widows find themselves with an insurance check larger than any amount of money they ever had in their lives. Don't tell everyone your business. You are not thinking clearly enough yet to loan your money to friends and relatives who think you hit the lottery. This is insurance money to help you survive financially, to help you get on your feet for the rest of your life, not to give away to people who find themselves in financial difficulties. Be selective, be careful, and take your time. When you figure out your financial situation, then you can start helping others, if you are able. And if you are comfortable, there is nothing wrong with sharing with those who need it.

Do not volunteer personal information over the telephone to strangers who call taking a survey. You never know who is legitimate. You are alone now, there are con artists out there ready to take advantage of a widow. Be careful.

I tried to do some things for "me" to make myself feel better. I had my hair done in a different style, a manicure, and a facial. I took bubble baths, read books and magazines. I tried to stimulate my mind and keep up with current events. I did some traveling. I became a volunteer at the hospital. I was patient with myself. I knew that someday I would be normal again and worked towards that goal.

Last but not least, hire a good lawyer. I could not have lived through any of this without my lawyer. I was very fortunate that I could trust him. He helped me and my children make decisions I would not have known how to make. I was still scared to make important decisions without Steve. He gave us advice and introduced me to people who were able to help with my financial decisions.

WHATEVER GETS YOU THROUGH THE NIGHT

◆

I was not interested in seeing anyone fall in love, fall out of love; make love or anything that had to do with love. I needed to laugh. Laughter was the only way to get me through the tears.

Insomnia was my enemy.

Because I was not accustomed to having the entire bed to myself, going to sleep alone at night was a challenge. For my bedroom, I purchased a new VCR and a new color TV with a sleep timer. I set the timer for two hours and fell asleep to the noise of the television every night. Just hearing the noise helped me sleep. I rented comedies, including all of the Jim Carey movies. I watched all of the old episodes of "Cheers" and "Taxi" television shows. I knew the entire line-up of "Nick at Night." I needed to watch anything that was not serious and especially programs that were not about romance. I was not interested in seeing anyone fall in love, fall out of love; make love or anything that had to do with love. I needed to laugh. Laughter was the only way to get me through the tears.

I was so tired of crying, my eyeballs were actually sore. Sometimes the sobbing was so hard that my heart physically hurt. I was in my late thirties and I was certain that I broke every blood vessel on my nose from blowing it so much.

I tried not to be afraid to look at pictures and videotapes of my husband. Although they were hard to see at first, they were very good for my healing process. I did not want to forget him.

I made photo collages, read old cards and letters, and listened to beautiful music. I went through all of our music and made special tapes of our favorite songs. I figured that sooner or later I would hear that special tune or see a photo or be reminded of him in some way. The more I got through now, the less set backs I would have down the road. I could not hide from my past. I could not pretend my life with Steve never existed.

Some people feel if they get rid of everything, sell the house and even move to a different city, the pain of loss will go away. It won't. Unless they board a spaceship to another planet, something somewhere on this earth will eventually remind them of their loved one. You can't escape. You must learn to deal with the sad tunes on the radio and even allow yourself to get choked up and cry. The next time you hear that special song, it will not hurt as much, and each time after, the pain will be less and less, and then one day you will hear that song and a little smile will form. Fond memories will replace the pain because you will have dealt with it.

It is okay to cry. When the last tear falls, you will feel better again. Someone once told me that God gave us tears to wash away the pain.

WHEN EVERYTHING JUST STOPPED

◆

I received his very last American Express bill a month after he died. The last date on the bill was Sept 8th. That date and the sequence number of 427 will follow me through the rest of my life.

For some reason, it was important for me to know every detail of my husband's final day on earth. I received his very last American Express bill a month after he died. The last date on the bill was Sept 8th. That date and the sequence number of 427 will follow me through the rest of my life. Just staring at that date sent chills through my body. It was the day when everything just stopped.

I knew where he ate lunch. And I knew which company he rented a car from at the Chicago airport. But I wondered what he ate for his last meal. I hoped he ordered dessert. One never knows if the final morsel of food that slides down your throat is going to be the last time you taste it. I wanted to know if he ate alone or was he with a client. If he did eat lunch with a client, what was his mood? Did he say anything profound that I could hold on to for the rest of my life?

I wondered whom he sat next to on the airplane. The airlines supplied us with a seating chart, but for some reason, my husband's name was out in the aisle with a tiny star. He could have sat two different places. He sometimes upgraded his seat to first class at the last minute if there was an empty seat. According to the chart, there was an empty seat in first class. So he may have met his destiny, in first class. I would like to believe that because he always got a thrill out of sitting in first class. It made him feel special. Whenever he returned from a business trip, he'd unpack his bag and toss me a bag of nuts. If they were peanuts, I knew he was in coach. If they were cashews, then he was in first class! It was a private little joke between the two of us. Unfortunately amongst his personal effects, there were no nuts. Maybe he was hungry and ate them. So I really don't know where he sat. I wondered if he spoke to the person seated next to him. When they knew something was wrong with the airplane, did they hold hands to comfort each other? Did he die feeling scared? Did he call out my name and the names of our children? Was he in terror? Did he pass out? I prayed that he fainted. Sometimes when he donated blood at the blood drive, he would pass out. I hung on to that hope, but the thing is, I will never really know.

There was a small plane crash in Georgia almost a year after ours, which fortunately had several survivors. I watched the news broadcast with concern and then with delight as this young man lived to tell his experience. I was ecstatic for him. The news showed his name and city across the screen. I hurried and wrote it on a piece of paper. About a week later, I called Directory Assistance and obtained his phone number. I telephoned him and explained that I had lost my husband on the USAir flight 427 in Pittsburgh. He said he remembered hearing about it, but didn't pay too much attention, and then almost immediately apologized and assured me that from now on, he would be more aware of such tragedies.

He offered me his sympathy on the death of my husband and I offered him my happiness that he had survived. I told him I was sorry to bother him, I was certain he was becoming inundated with telephone calls. He laughed and said he thought perhaps after a week his "fifteen minutes" were over. I laughed, and decided not to warn him that it might not be over just yet!

"Are you married?" I asked.

"Yes" he answered.

"Do you have any children?"

"Yes I do." He said very proudly.

"Good!" I said. "I really need to ask you something. I hope it's not too personal, or too difficult for you to talk about, but I have always wondered what went through my husband's mind before the plane crashed."

This man, this complete stranger, who didn't know me from Adam, was kind enough to share his last thoughts before the plane went down. He must have sensed how imperative it was for me to know. Perhaps he even thought about how important it would have been for him to have his wife and children know what his thoughts were had he not survived.

"Well," he took a deep breath, "I must admit, when the plane was going down, the flight attendant instructed us to put our heads on our laps. I thought…this is it! I really thought I was going to die. I truly did not think I would survive. I thought about my wife and my children. Although I felt happy that they knew how much I loved them, I was so sad that my children would have to go through their lives without a father. My last thoughts were of my family"

I was tearing up as he continued.

"When I actually woke up, I could not believe I was alive. You can be sure I will never take life for granted now."

He sounded so happy. So rejuvenated.

"Live life to the fullest now," I said to him with a little smile. "You are a very fortunate man and your wife and children are very lucky."

I thanked him and told him that now I was sure my husband thought about my kids and me. I wished him well, hung up the telephone, and cried. Why couldn't my husband have been the one to survive too?

I knew Steve was tired that afternoon, having to awaken so early in the morning. Maybe he was quiet that day on the airplane and was reading one of his paperback novels. He was a Stephen King fan, and recently was reading Dean Koontz. I found one of his paperback books on the bookshelf months after the crash. Ironically it had a boarding pass as a bookmark and the flight number was the same, USAir 427 from Chicago. It gave me this uneasy feeling. I wondered how many other times he flew that same flight from Chicago. I had this urge to find out.

I went through his day timer to see how many other times he made the same trip. I found another paperback book with another boarding pass used as a bookmark. The life of a traveling businessman. He used boarding passes for bookmarks.

I sat on the floor holding his book looking at the bookmark. The realization that he would not know how the story ended made me sad. I latched onto my faith and thought if everything I was taught was true, then he now lived in the ultimate place where he knows all of the answers. Maybe he really does already know the end of this paperback book, as he might with all books, with all life.

I was confused. I did not know if I should feel sad for him, happy for him, or jealous. Because now if he was in this ultimate paradise known to us as Heaven, and he had no more pain or heartache or guilt, no more money worries, or worried about the fate of our children and things like calories from double chocolate fudge ice cream and balances from check-books didn't matter anymore and he just floated around and jumped from one heavenly place to another feeling all peaceful and fulfilled, then why was I the one stuck behind with all the pain, responsibility and grief? What did I do wrong in this life to be so punished? Sometimes the bitter pain replaced the sad pain. And sometimes that was a good thing and sometimes it wasn't. Nobody said grieving was easy.

VALIDATION

◆

I needed to hear…"Yes, you were dealt a rotten hand. Yes, it is unfair that you and Steve, who were so in love, won't grow old together, won't spoil your grandchildren together and won't go on that second honeymoon.

What I wanted more than anything from everyone was "validation."

It is necessary to educate family and friends on how to deal with someone who has lost a spouse. Please do not tell me you know what it is like not to have a spouse because your husband goes away on a two day business trip, once every other month! You do not know what it is like. And please do not insult me by saying that I am so lucky because I do not have to cook dinner anymore or iron his shirts or worry about him driving through a snowstorm.

And those who are divorced please do not tell me that your experience was "like" a death and you know exactly how I feel! I did not choose to be single. He did not choose to die! There was no preparation and no trial separation. We still wanted to be together. Please do not tell me that his dying is better than a divorce. Do you really think I get solace knowing that my husband did not want to leave me? No, it hurts even more. Because I do not even have the right to be angry with him because the only mistake he made was getting on the wrong airplane. There is a difference!

I needed to hear…"Yes, you were dealt a rotten hand. Yes, it is unfair that you and Steve who were so in love, won't grow old together, won't spoil your grandchildren together, won't go on that second honeymoon, won't see Europe, Hawaii, or even the Grand Canyon together." I wanted them to say, "Yes you really have a load on your shoulders with the responsibility of the kids now that you are all alone. How can I help?"

I needed validation to assure myself that what I was feeling was normal. I needed everyone to understand that when I had to leave a holiday dinner or a party after a brief time, to think before they try and bully me into staying by making me feel guilty by calling me a party-pooper. I needed them to realize how much strength it took for me to just get there. Seeing the usual crowd having an enjoyable time, knowing that my partner is visibly missing was difficult. Remembering a time when he was there standing among everyone, smiling and laughing, thinking of the witty things he would be saying, always brought tears to my eyes, a lump in my throat and a pain like a knife right through my heart.

When all of the conversations are taking place, I no longer had that special someone to go stand beside or hold onto or even look across the room for anymore. There were no more private winks or feelings of comfort from my partner. When I passed on an invitation to something I felt I could not handle, I wished everyone had been a little more patient and understanding. I wish they could have put themselves in my shoes just for a little while and imagine driving to a function and walking in all alone.

Sometimes well meaning people say things without thinking…or knowing. There was an occasion when five of us widow's decided to take an airplane trip together to Las Vegas. I wanted to visit with my brother and his family and they wanted to see a few shows.

We managed to sit all across one row together along with another woman, our age that was flying alone. After about thirty minutes of our chattering over her head, she became part of our conversation. She and her husband were both flying to Las Vegas for a few days without their children. She said every time they fly somewhere her husband takes another plane in case the plane crashes. This way their children would still have at least one parent. She was laughing, telling us how she thought her husband was so silly.

Well, the five of us widows looked at each other and warned with our eyes *not* to tell this woman our story. Three and a half hours short of landing isn't the right time to tell someone our tragedy. She asked us how we got so lucky to leave the husbands at home and have a "girls only vacation!" We just pleasantly smiled and didn't know how to answer. She kept asking us questions like if our husbands worked together, or if we were all friends for a long time. Finally one of the widows quietly told her our story. The next minute I looked over at the woman and she was crying into a hanky. I felt terrible for her. She looked at all of us and just sobbed. She said she heard about the crash, of course, being from Pittsburgh and she didn't know how we all had the strength to go on. Suddenly her husband's idea of taking different flights didn't seem so silly anymore. The five of us felt uneasy for her because she was totally uncomfortable for the duration of the flight. When the plane landed she literally raced up the aisle and ran down the ramp…into her husband's arms I am sure.

The worst insult however, was when people would tell me that enough time had passed and I should be "over it" by now. Some experts tell us that after two years, we should start feeling normal again. I guarantee you that on the two-year mark, magical dust does not fall down upon us and make the pain suddenly disappear. It happens very gradually and differently to everyone. Everyone grieves at his or her own speed. Some people need many years and others may never recover. My grandmother never recovered from my grandfather's death. For seventeen years she missed him and mourned him every single day. Whenever anyone would allow her, she talked about him with such love and such pain still in her eyes.

Something that I also experienced after the death of my husband was that certain people who I was in contact with before he died, for some reason, had no idea what to say to me. So they said nothing. They did nothing. They ignored my family and me as though we had some sort of epidemic and they did not want to be next. There would be occasions when I would see these particular people at a shopping mall and out of the corner of my eye, I would watch them hurry and turn the other way. I had much more respect for those who came face to face with me and simply admitted that they just didn't know what to say. I would put them at ease. I understood. I suppose some people are afraid of saying the wrong thing, so they say nothing. Personally, I appreciated those who were honest and sympathetic and just said, "I don't know what to say, but I am here if you need anything."

I learned how important it is to write a little note inside a sympathy card instead of just signing my name. I read every single card we received. All of the notes were touching and comforting. Especially those who mentioned my husband and told a special little story that reminded them about him.

A woman who knew my husband when he was a young boy wrote me a beautiful letter and sent me some pictures of him. I received notes and cards from business associates that I never met, telling me how Steve always talked about his wife and his children. A receptionist at his dentist's office wrote and told me that of all the many busy executives, Steve was one who always called and canceled an appointment when something came up, never leaving them waiting. He was a conscientious man. Those notes meant more to me than a big basket of flowers or fruit.

Something else we all need to remember is that there is no competition for grief. I lost a husband. My children lost a father. My mother-in-law lost a son. My brother-in-laws lost a brother. Steve's friends lost a buddy. Everyone hurt. Everyone was affected by his death.

Although there really shouldn't be a monopoly on grief, I will probably always contend that losing a spouse is the worst thing in the world simply because my entire life as I knew it, changed. The man I called my partner, my best friend, my lover, was no longer there. I would have to learn how to live all over again and watch my children graduate from college, get married, and grow into adulthood without him beside me sharing the joy. Everyone else could return to their normal lives while my life was to be changed on a daily basis. The void, the empty chair at the kitchen table, the empty side of our bed was present everyday for me. There was no escaping my grief. Is it fair to say my pain was more then my children's pain, more than his mother's or more than his brother's? Is it right for them to think that I can someday go on and get remarried and replace him, but they will never be able to replace a father, a son and a brother?

I think with all respect that this special man touched all of our lives in different ways and we need to realize that we all grieve him differently. If I do decide someday to allow myself to have another intimate relationship, it will not mean that I no longer loved my spouse. We should respect one another's loss and not compete for the grief. And until we walk in each other's shoes, never ever judge.

SUPPORT

◆

I will never forget the first time I went to a support group meeting. I looked around the room and saw other grieving spouses from the plane crash and the first thing that came to my mind was, "This is the OTHER side of the plane."

In Pittsburgh, the Allegheny County Health department set up a support group for the family members to attend for emotional support. There were several locations in different sections of the city to make it easy for us to attend these support group meetings. Because of this effort, several of us decided to form the "427 Air Disaster Support League" (ADSL). This would allow us to continue supporting one another and enable our group to do many other things pertaining to air safety and memorial services for the families of flight 427.

I will never forget the first time I went to a support group meeting. I looked around the room and saw all of the other grieving spouses from the plane crash and the first thing that came to my mind was, "This is the *other* side of the plane." Everyone had the same distraught, lost, shocked look on their faces as I did. With this group, for the first time since the crash, I finally felt at home. I was with people who knew exactly how I felt. I was among a kindership.

I was fortunate to have been part of a support group with other 427 plane crash family members and spouses. I value my special friendships with all of them. Since our group in the north section of the city was so big, they decided it would be best to separate the spouses from the other members of the families. This way we would be able to communicate about being a widow or widower easily with one another. I thought it was a great idea because I felt that losing a spouse brought different concerns then losing an adult child or parent or sibling. Although everyone has a right to grieve, I think it was best to be around those who were in the same or similar situation.

We would meet and listen and affirm one another's fears and congratulate each other's accomplishments. In the beginning, we would talk about our spouses, our crushed dreams, how we coped suddenly being single. We were a group of lost souls given another script to follow. We belonged to a club that no one wanted to join. But together through the weeks, months, and years, we have cried with each other, laughed with each other, encouraged each other, and have applauded each other. The facilitators of these groups had their hands full. I don't think they ever encountered such a group before. But they were strong for our sake and allowed us to speak freely without offering us too much advice. They gave us the opportunity to meet with each other. For that, I will always be grateful.

After the allotted time with the Allegheny County Health Department was over, we would continue on our own to meet for lunch or dinners and later on, evening get-to-gethers.

We have stood next to one other during memorial services of the airplane crash, an emotional funeral of a fellow widow, memorial golf tournaments, engagements and weddings and college graduations. Some of us have traveled together, exchanged dating tips, and even spent holidays and special occasions together.

Forming the 427 ADSL enabled us to attend the National Transportation Safety Board (N.T.S.B.) hearings in January 1995 after the plane crash. It was the first time in history that the N.T.S.B. set aside special seating for the family members. At the end of the hearings, Chairman, Jim Hall would talk with us, assuring everyone that he would do everything he could to find the cause of this airplane crash. The county coroner came to a special meeting with family members only, no cameras or media and answered all of our questions. We were a group now. There is something to be said about strength in numbers. Slowly but surely, we would become stronger.

There was one special widow in particular, who no matter where we may live will be one of my best friends for the rest of my life. We will always be there for one another no matter what happens. She and I were each other's validation on many occasions and we helped one another from losing our minds. There were many late nights on the telephone when we were either to scared to sleep or insomnia kicked in. We supported each other through the media limelight at the N.T.S.B. hearings, birthday's, wedding anniversaries and holidays. We assured one another that what we were feeling was normal.

I was the first person to make her laugh again one evening at a Chinese Restaurant while we were eating fried rice. We were discussing what we thought our purpose was now on Earth and wondered what our husband's would think about their "little housewives" appearing on national television, making semi-intelligent statements to the newspapers, and meeting the head of the N.T.S.B. Feeling somewhat comedic, I gave her my rendition of a conversation that I thought our husbands were having up in heaven. She laughed so loud; her daughter came over to our table and commented how refreshing it was to hear her mom laugh again.

We were good for each other's morale. We often joked that both of our husband's must be up in heaven laughing together at some of the adventures their wives have encountered! From the beginning there seemed to have been a spiritual connection between the two of us widows. We always made the other feel better and snapped each other back to reality. We joked that our husbands probably met first, compared notes on wives and children and decided that somehow, some way, they needed the two of us to bond and help each other. It worked.

Although six years have gone by, some of us still meet for dinners and lunches and keep in constant communication via e-mail and telephone. The support we have given one another helped the healing process tremendously.

Each year on the anniversary of the airplane crash, we stand together at the Sewickley Cemetery in front of the giant memorial listening to poems or encouraging scriptures read by some of the families. There are spouses, parents, children, siblings, relatives and friends who come from all over the country. As the names of our loved ones are called out in a familiar tribute, someone from the family places a flower on the memorial. I still close my eyes tightly in disbelief when I hear my husband's name. This yearly ritual is something we will probably continue to do for as long as we find necessary. It is our way to let our loved ones know that we still love them, think about them, and will never forget them.

I applaud all of the family members for surviving one of the worst public tragedies. I wrote this before and I will say it again. On September 8th 1994 when they continuously announced there were no survivors from USAir flight 427, they were wrong. *We* are the survivors.

SIGNS, SPIRITS AND THINGS THAT GO BUMP IN THE NIGHT

◆

There have been times when I would hold his wedding ring and pray for added strength to help me through a problem, and like magic, it would work.

Because my husband's death was so tragically instant, I needed to know if his spirit, full of energy, could totally disappear so quickly from earth and from my life.

I visited several psychics hoping that like in the movie *Ghost*, Steve would be able to contact me through a spiritual medium a la Whoppi Goldberg. Always skeptical, I wondered if these psychics really saw anything besides the twenty-dollar bill I handed them at the end of the hour.

But I have to admit there were some things that occurred that needed no explaining and I began to question coincidences and spiritual divine interventions. I am convinced that there were some occurrences that were just too on target to be coincidental. Before you send those nice young men in their clean white coats to take me away to the funny farm, keep an open mind.

Exactly one week after the accident, I had a dream about Steve. I saw what he looked like as the airplane was descending. His hair was blowing back and terror was upon his face. It was almost what you would see on the downhill ride of a very fast roller coaster; only there was no smile. As I saw the terror on his face in my dream, everything went black. I could actually feel his arms tighten around me. I was partly asleep and partly awake. In my mind, I was frightened of the feeling and I said, "Please stop this, you are scaring me!" Suddenly I woke completely up, out of breath. I decided to go downstairs and get some fresh air. I opened the sliding glass doors to our enclosed patio and then opened the screen doors to allow the fresh air inside. I happened to glance down on the ground in front of the doors. Overnight-appeared vines of clinging ivy from one end of the patio enclosure to the other, much like a protective shield to guard our home. Being a lover of plants and nature, this was Steve's favorite room in the whole house. For hours he would sit in this room watching the birds and the squirrels fighting over the bird feeder. He would stare through the wooded tree area and drink his coffee and read the newspaper.

Everyone in the family who came over that day looked at the vines in amazement. It was a miracle because we knew the vines were not there the day before. They appeared out of nowhere, over night, instantly. I took photographs not knowing how long they would last. They survived through the winter and the snow and are still there. Green as can be. I had a man who studied biology look at the vines. He said they were called "clinging ivy." He also said he did not know how they remained so green during the winter underneath all that snow. I just smiled.

Do I think Steve had something to do with that? Yes I do. I believe he was trying to reach me and this was the only way his spirit could let me know that he was still around protecting his family. I felt a sense of peace and security knowing that he was somewhere out there watching us.

There would be many more instances of the spiritual act that would occur over the next few years. Is it wrong for us to think that our loved ones can actually have higher power to grant us the favors that we ask? I don't know. All I do know is that there have been times when I would hold on to his wedding ring and pray for added strength to help me through a problem, and like magic, it would work. There are times when I just whispered a "thank you" and don't question the higher power, whatever it may be. Some say it is our guardian angel, some say it is God. I won't dispute anything at this point. I am just grateful for being heard.

Special songs that played on the radio during certain times of depression led me to believe that my husband was sending me a sign for me to know he was still around and that he still loved me. There were mornings when I would quickly awaken before the alarm, and suddenly the FM station on the clock radio would turn on and the music would be a favorite song of ours. I would smile and knew if he could protect us, he would.

A few months after he died, I was driving my daughter on the Pennsylvania Turnpike to visit a potential college. It was storming and the rain was pouring so severely, I could barely see through the windshield. I was upset that her father wasn't there to help with this important endeavor and then became even angrier that I had to be the one driving on the turnpike in this torrential downpour. I was afraid we were going to be in an accident. My daughter sat quietly beside me with terror on her face. I was sure she was thinking the same thing. If her father was here, he would be driving and we would both feel safer. There are just some things that a father does better than a mother and driving on the turnpike in a downpour was Steve's job. Not mine.

I became angrier and through my tears and through the rain smacking against the windshield I began mentally talking to Steve. I told him this was not fair. He should have been here driving, not me. We had these children together and I should not have to deal with all of this alone. It was difficult enough that we had to visit this college and be around all of the other students with both sets of parents, constantly feeling like half of a family. I was secretly scolding him with all of my might. Within half of a minute, the rain suddenly stopped. I could see again. I took a deep breath and looked over at my daughter who also displayed a look of relief. Then the sun came through. We both smiled.

I whispered a silent "thank you" several times. Was it a coincidence? I didn't care. I was just so grateful I could drive the rest of the way safely. But, I needed to believe he was around. I still needed him. We all did.

There have been so many other signs that I had never experienced before my husband's death. I cannot ignore them. Maybe God thought Steve's job on Earth was finished. I didn't think he was finished. I still think it was a huge mistake that my husband changed his flight at the last minute and walked onto the airplane of doom. He wasn't supposed to be there. We still had many years of living to do together. I am certain that like in the movie, "Heaven Can Wait" Steve tried over and over again to explain to God that he needed to jump back into his body and get back to his family. I am certain that my husband fought with all of his might to come back to us. Only there wasn't a body to jump back into. Perhaps that is why God allowed him to keep a close watch over us. His time wasn't supposed to be up.

Who was I to question God? Was there a God? What kind of a God would allow someone so sweet and good to be taken from those he loved? All I knew was that I was a young widow left with the responsibility of finishing to raise our children alone. It was a task I did not ask for. Nor did I want. If Steve was peacefully floating around up in heaven, enjoying the tranquility of the angels and attaining all of the knowledge he wished he knew when he was here, I certainly was not going to remain quiet down on Earth. When I needed him, I was going to call loud and clear for him to hear. I would disturb him, amuse him, and pray for him to continue to help our children and me. It reminds me of what Peter Pan always said about Tinker bell. We need to believe. And believe I did.

I don't abuse it. I choose my requests very carefully.

LONELINESS

◆

There is no longer that one person there to tell everything, to share everything, to buy a Valentines Day card or an Anniversary present. The enjoyment of sharing your life with just one special person is gone.

You feel alone in a world full of people.

Welcome to Widowhood.

It is very difficult to suddenly find yourself alone amongst a world full of couples. There is nothing wrong with those who prefer to be single. They chose to live alone. When you lose a spouse to death, you did not choose to walk this earth with no one beside you. Suddenly you go from "Honey, I'm home," to silence.

There is no longer that special person there to tell everything, to share everything, to buy a Valentine's Day card or an Anniversary present. The enjoyment of sharing your life with just one special person is gone.

Living alone means zipping up your own zipper on the back of your dress with great difficulty. It means fastening your bracelets one handed with a mouthful of teeth, rubbing your own feet after hours in high-heeled shoes, scratching your own back, and having to change the toilet paper in your master bathroom because no one else is there but you.

Alone at night when you hear a thump on the roof, there isn't anyone next to you to assure you that you are hearing noises and insists for you to go back to sleep. Alone in the dark, rainstorms and thunderstorms and howling winds are much more ferocious. But you know when the rain subsides and the sun rises the birds will chirp announcing another day, putting to rest that a burglar was on top of the house last night while you laid awake with the light on, counting the flowers in the border on the wall.

Being held, kissed, touched, and making love are now gone. You put your sexuality on the shelf. At 38, I thought I would be celibate for the rest of my life. I could not even think about being a woman ever again. Then, as time went on and I began to think, "Hey, it's been six whole months, or nine whole months and then one whole year since I've made love." Moe, Larry and Curly begin to look pretty good at three in the morning during one of those insomnia attacks while watching late night TV.

How do you handle these certain feelings? You are very careful not to watch certain romantic movies for fear that those feelings will begin to stir and he's not there to release the tension. I am sure I could have gone to a bar or a club and gone home with a stranger and did the deed and release the frustration but I know myself and that would not have been sufficient. I am the dinner and a movie, what's your favorite color kind of girl. I would have felt more awful after the deed than before so I stayed clear of sexual promiscuity and decided to wait for the right man...again.

I was married for twenty years and we enjoyed a very normal healthy sexual love for one another. Now it was cut off. Being a single woman in the nineties threw me. I was never single. I was always with Steve. My self-esteem and self-confidence blew up in that airplane crash with my husband. I no longer had that constant male figure telling me that I looked nice or that I smelled good.

I did not know the latest dating protocol and I was not only very old fashioned but had regressed to the mental dating age of about fifteen years old. So now I was in my late thirties with the dating mentality younger than my daughter. And besides the "Three Stooges" looking sexy to me, I began feeling extremely frustrated in the sex department. I remember standing behind a man in line at the supermarket and being only inches away from him. I could smell his cologne and just for a split second I had this urge to touch his shoulders and run my fingers through his hair. It was awful.

All I can say is do what you need to do. Rent movies, buy magazines, and pretend you are with Brad Pitt, Mel Gibson, Paul Newman or all three…until you are ready to make love again with another human being, do as they do in Rome…

When you do find that someone special and you do feel you are ready to make love again, don't be surprised if you can't go through with it, or if you feel guilty because you can, and even guiltier because you enjoyed it and didn't feel guilty. When the time is right, it can be good again. It will be good again. With the right person! Be patient.

WHEN WILL I FEEL NORMAL AGAIN?

◆

I wanted a month, day and time for this auspicious occasion.

I am a "Bottom line" woman, typically by nature a very impatient person. I do not like to waste time. So from the very beginning, all I wanted to know was "When will I feel normal again?" I wanted a month, day and time for this auspicious occasion.

I remember the very first time I went grocery shopping after my husband died. Out of habit, I wanted to place things in the cart that I would normally purchase every week for Steve. I realized that I didn't need to buy Cranapple Juice anymore, or Oreo Double Stuffed cookies, and when it came time to pass the cereal aisle, I looked at his favorite cereal and wanted to cry. I left the shopping cart in the middle of the aisle and quickly walked out of the store.

I had a difficult time going into any restaurants that we used to frequent near our home. Just the aroma of the food made me physically ill. Seeing another man with a similar build wearing a dark suit or a black leather jacket made me yearn for my husband. I could not look at any men with white shirts and ties for the longest time. I had a difficult time shopping at the mall, especially the men's department. Walking past the ties and the men's dress shirts made me want to cry. I used to buy his clothes. That privilege was taken away from me. It hurt. I didn't think I could ever walk through the men's department again. But I did. And each time I walked through the store the pain hurt less and less.

It was the immediate pain I needed to get through. Unless I was willing to move away from all of the places that brought back memories, I needed to face them head on and hold my breath as best as I could and get through it. Sometimes I just couldn't and that was all right. I would leave the situation and go home where I felt safe.

I knew that eventually I had to go back into that grocery store and shop for food again. To think I would not was unrealistic. I also knew that I wanted to return to some of those restaurants too. And I did. And each time I went, it got easier and easier. Now I whiz in and out of that same grocery store and don't even think about purchasing "Cocoa Puffs." And the restaurants are easy now too.

Pretend for example that you need to cross a large lake. In order to get to the other side, you must follow a path of rocks. You will need to step on top of every large rock. You cannot skip over certain stages of grief just like you cannot skip over any of the rocks in the lake. You must land right on top of each one. Stand there for a while with all of your weight, take a deep breath and then go on to the next rock. Take one step at a time. Skipping over a rock only prolongs the healing process. I assure you, if you ignore the grief now, or skip over any part of the process, someday, somewhere, down the road it will come back. In order to get over the grief, you need to go through it. You will have to deal with it eventually. It is so much better to get through it now so you can get on with your life. So just think of healing as crossing that lake. Take each step, one step at a time.

Eight months after my husband died, I talked with my uncle. Thirty-some years earlier he lost my aunt who was twenty-nine years old at the time and my cousin who was only three in a tragic automobile accident. My uncle had since married and had more children. I asked him, "Uncle Jack, how did you ever get over it? How did you go on?" We now had this connection called tragedy that bonded us.

He looked straight at me, shook his head, and tenderly said, "You will never get over this. You will never forget Steve…and you shouldn't. He will always be a part of you. You will learn to live with it and you will learn to add on to your life. You will just add on.

"How long, Uncle Jack, how long until I can feel somewhat normal again?"

Again he shook his head not wanting to be pinned down to a certain time limit, but he saw the desperation in my eyes, I had been a widow for only eight months. "Give yourself a good two years. Maybe less…maybe more."

I learned not to expect that magical dust to come pouring over me and take away the pain by a certain date. Grief knows nothing of time. It comes and goes at its leisure. I knew that I had to allow the time to mend. I've learned the toughest lesson of all: to be patient with myself. Once I realized that I was doing the best I could, I began to mend noticeably. We do have the power within us to do almost anything. It is learning how to use that power wisely and efficiently that will help us.

JOURNALIZE YOUR THOUGHTS

◆

Every once in a while I will flip back and read what I wrote and realize how much I have progressed.

Even if you only write the day, the date, the time and the words, "I felt crappy again today." Write. Write. Write. Write for yourself.

Remember, no English teacher or college professor is going to circle misspelled words or incorrect grammar with a red ink pen. There is no grade on this. But in time as you progress, and you will progress, that "I felt crappy today" will eventually turn into, "I didn't have THAT bad of a day."

Because Steve was my best friend and he was no longer there on a daily basis to tell my news to, or my deep personal thoughts and fears, I used my journal. This book became my best friend. Sometimes I would talk to Steve through the writings, especially when I was mad because he was no longer here to help with certain situations. Every once in a while I will flip back and read my journal and realize how much I progressed. I am proud of my improvement. Writing is a cathartic process. Just getting it out and off your chest will make you feel better.

Sometimes when I read what I wrote, I realize what a different person I am now. I am much stronger. When I read how much pain I was in, I breathe a sigh of relief that I no longer feel so desperate. It reinforces the fact that I am getting better. I have come a long way.

I highly recommend keeping a journal. Write in it as often as you need. You will be surprised that when you are having good days, you will not need to write anything. That is a good sign!

WHO AM I NOW?

◆

Although legally I was still Mrs. Shortley, in my heart there was no Mr. Shortley and I felt awkward using that title. How can you be a Mrs. without a Mr.? That is what I thought, anyway.

I am as much for equal rights as any independent woman. However, I was as proud being "Steve's wife", as he was being "my husband." I cherished being introduced as his wife. I loved hearing him proudly announce to people, "This is *my* wife!" I was a wife for twenty years. It was a title I lavished in. Now I was no longer a wife, I was no longer a Mrs. either. Although legally I was still Mrs. Shortley, in my heart there was no Mr. Shortley and I felt awkward using that title. How can you be a Mrs. without a Mr.? That is what I thought, anyway.

There were several occasions when salespeople would refer to my husband, not knowing he was deceased. Sometimes I would not say anything and just pretend that he was still alive. If I were to tell this stranger that my husband passed away, I would need to explain, because I still looked too young to be a widow and I would watch their faces grow into deep concern and the entire situation would go from something pleasant to something uncomfortable. All I really wanted to do was purchase some furniture or a car or something simple. If I hesitated they would say, "Oh, you have to check with the hubby?" or "Bring your hubby back with you if you want."

I would overhear other wives talking about their husbands and yearn for that privilege again. I wanted to add to the conversation too, but it would always have to be in the past tense now and that would just make everyone else feel ill at ease, so I would just keep my thoughts to myself. I no longer belonged in that circle anymore. I wasn't prepared for this dethroning of my title. I still wanted to be a wife.

The first time I filled out a form that needed the marital status checked, I resented having to check the little box that read "widowed." I didn't like being referred to as a widow! I pouted and checked single. Sometimes I checked the married box, because in my heart, I still was. Then I would erase it and check single. It would take me five minutes to just complete that section of the form!

Did I need to remove my wedding rings? I loved my wedding rings. I knew some widows who wore their wedding rings for years. (Remember my Grandmother? She died wearing her ring) I continued to wear mine for a whole year. Then one day I decided that I really was not married anymore. I removed them. I still loved my diamond, so I had it made to fit on my right hand. I had my husband's wedding band returned to its circular shape and had it soldered with my anniversary diamond ring and I wear it on another finger. Again, this is something totally left up to the individual. I placed my wedding band, the ring that was part of me for twenty years, into my safe.

Something else that many widows lose is the status of their husband's work. For many years they accompany their spouses to all of their work related dinners, parties and summer picnics making friends with all of the co-workers and their spouses. Suddenly, they are no longer a part of those activities. They lose contact with those people and it would become as though they never even existed. In my case I was a reminder of something unpleasant, the accidental tragic death of a co-worker.

HOLIDAYS, BIRTHDAYS
AND ANNIVERSARIES

◆

I would go through the boxes of decorations and find Steve's Christmas stocking and the ornaments with his name and not know what to do with them. I would hold them and cry.

Holidays used to be a festive occasion in our home. I would decorate the inside of the house with beautiful Christmas displays while Steve decorated the outside of the house with little white twinkle lights. The first Christmas after he died, I did not want to celebrate the season. I had no magical holiday feeling. I could not imagine how I was going to get through Christmas and then New Years Eve without the man I had been spending these special occasions with for the past two decades.

I had no desire to shop or buy presents. I did not want to receive any gifts either. The only present that I wanted was my husband. Walking through the festively decked shopping malls listening to Christmas carols, watching people scurry about, knowing they would be going home to their normal happy cookie-scented holiday households made my eyes tear up with sadness. If I did not have my children, I would have taken a flight to some deserted island until January 2nd. It was unbearable.

For the first two Christmas seasons, I would go through the boxes of decorations and find Steve's Christmas stocking and the ornaments with his name and not know what to do with them. I would hold them and cry. Then gently put them back into the box. The third Christmas, I cried a little less and put the ornaments on the tree. But I still placed all of our stockings back into the box. I did not want to hang his stocking and yet, I did not want to hang mine and my children's without his. There would have been a visible void seeing just three where there used to hang four. I thought it best to put all of them back into the attic.

Once we thought our children were old enough, our family adopted a tradition of opening presents from each other on Christmas Eve so we could sleep in the morning. That first year, just three months after the plane crash, my children and I tried with all of our might to maintain that tradition with just the three of us. I felt it was important that we remain a family no matter how difficult it was for the three of us to continue without the fourth major part of our household. Sad and pathetic are two words that come to my mind to describe the three of us exchanging gifts and trying to pretend this was a festive occasion. We were three souls on the ship of life lost without our captain. I had to take over the captain's role because I knew they were looking to follow me now. Thing is, I was in no shape to lead. I dreaded this festivity as much as them.

Lisa, Dan and me had so much empathy and love for one another that somehow we made it through the exchange. None of us were really thrilled to unwrap presents, but we went through the motions. We all went to bed that night knowing that at least we tried.

The next morning as they lay sleeping, I woke up early, dressed in winter attire and grabbed my Walkman and went for a long brisk cold walk. The Doors singing, "Break on through to the other side" blasting through my ears. I tried not to look in any of the windows of all the houses as I passed by, wondering what joyful excitement was happening at that very moment with all the little children gleefully opening Santa's presents. That was all my life used to's. I felt so sorry for the three of us. Happy days were all in the past now.

I think the first New Years Eve was the toughest of the holidays. Like Valentine's Day it is an evening for "couples." Well meaning friends may insist you need to be around other people but beware, when the giant ball in Time Square falls and the clock strikes midnight, he is not there to kiss while all the confetti is falling and the horns are blowing. I remember thinking to myself, "So this is it. This is my life now." I went into the ladies room at the restaurant and I cried. I hated it. I wished I had stayed home alone that first New Years Eve and watched a video on TV.

The next holiday was Valentine's Day. There were reminders everywhere about *"love."* I had to endure the radio and television commercials, and the newspapers all promoting Valentine's Day sales for special gifts of love. I thought for certain that my days of receiving long stemmed red roses were over. I couldn't go anywhere without feeling the emptiness. I resented not being able to purchase a Valentine's Day card for my husband. So I went to the card store and purchased one anyway. I brought it to the cemetery along with a heart shaped balloon that said, "I love you."

Then came Easter and once again reminders of years when we colored eggs together and prepared for Easter dinner. I had to endure the family dinner. My spouse no longer occupied the seat next to me. I would glance around the table and lose my appetite because I would think of Steve. But I kept a stiff upper lip for the sake of the children and everyone else.

Then it was my birthday. It just seemed like there was one event after another that we had to go through. I remember the first time buying my daughter a birthday card. It was one month after my husband died. In the card shop, I reached for a pretty card and realized I could not purchase it because it said "To *our* daughter" I was no longer an "our." I choked back my tears and resented that I had to now purchase a card that just simply read, "daughter."

Our wedding anniversary was another difficult day. Every year we went out for a special dinner. That first year after he died, I drove to the site where the plane had crashed, parked and walked into the peaceful wooded area, sat down on a beach towel and wrote Steve a four page letter. I always felt that the crash site was some sacred place because one hundred and thirty-two people died right on that land:

June 14th 1995

"Flag Day…black flag day for me. It's our 21st wedding anniversary. Instead of sitting in a lovely restaurant as we always did, I'm sitting here all alone on an old towel in the middle of a forest in Hopewell Township…also known as "the crash site."

Happy Anniversary Steve.

I wonder if I'll be doing this little ritual every year on Flag Day for the rest of my life-however long that may be. Shoot. I forgot to bring tissues and I am already starting to tear up. I have my car keys, my camera, (you know I always bring my camera with me!) and my new toy, a cellular phone. But no damn tissues. I'm sitting here looking at our tree.

On February 14th, I was here with two other 427 widowers. I picked a tree that day and tacked a laminated heart with our picture onto it. Today below the heart, in honor of our Flag Day Anniversary, I placed a flag. Someday that tree will be full of stuff just for you, Steve.

So. This is where you died? I look around all these trees; these beautiful trees and I wonder why such a devastating accident had to happen to so many good people. It's funny I don't feel death here. I don't feel spooked either. I feel complacent. And a nice summer breeze. Quiet.

You'd have liked this place. It would have made a nice place for a camping trip. I could see you sitting on your chair with your book, beer and ciggie-butts…and your cheese curls. I miss you Steve. I still cry every day. Sometimes I don't even know why. But it's every day.

I wish you'd give me some sign that everything's gonna be okay. I'm afraid of losing it. I wish I had some Kleenex now. I'm crying. Flooding tears. Sometimes I still can't believe this happened to you. I tell myself I'm in a dream sequence of an Alfred Hitchcock movie. Any minute I'll wake up next to you and say: "Gees, Steve, you won't believe the dream I had!"

It's not going to happen though, is it? I'm trying to go on. I think I can if you help me. But I need a sign.

It would have been a happy 21st if you had not died. Why did you have to go to Chicago that morning? Of all days, of all flights. Boy Steve, you really picked a loser 9/8/94.

I know you had no idea. I don't blame you for all this pain. I truly don't. If they would have told you the plane was going to crash into a million pieces, and you were never going to see the kids and me again, I know you would have walked home from Chicago.

I wonder what went through your mind. You must have been so scared, huh? I hope you didn't suffer. I hope for your sake it was instant, just like my dream. You always told me you'd never leave me. You promised me forever. Is forever till death do us part? Is there something or someone else out there for me now? I don't know Steve, but if you have anything to do with my rest of my life, you better make it good! If I have to suffer any more pain and loneliness for the rest of my earthly days, when I get to heaven and join you, I will yell at you so loud, all the other angels will fly south! (I'm just joking!)

I wonder what it is you do after you die. Nine months is such a long time. Are you a bird? Are you a seagull? Did you know that I went to South Carolina? Did you follow me to Las Vegas? God I wish I knew. I cried last night as soon as the clock struck 12:01. I can't wait until today is over, then June 14th will be over."

It was something that I needed to do. I have a notebook and on every wedding anniversary, I go someplace different and write him a letter. Just to sort of update on what has been happening. I don't know how long I will continue this ritual. But it is my small way of remembering my first wedding to my first love.

The second year of holidays, birthdays and anniversaries was just a little bit easier. It did not hurt as much as the first year, but the vacancy was still very much apparent. At least in the second year, I had a little more of a desire to decorate again and participate in some of the festivities.

By the time the third year came, something occurred that would begin to change the way I would feel about holidays. Thanksgiving Day was approaching and I was feeling sorry for myself. Holidays were always the worst. This would be the third Thanksgiving without my husband. Even though I had my children and a huge family to spend the holiday with, I was beginning to feel anxiety spending another holiday without Steve and the normalcy of a complete family again. I received a Thanksgiving card from a widower friend of mine who had lost his wife in a car accident. He wrote:

"You and I have been through quite a bit these past years and through tragedy we still have many things to be thankful for…We may have lost loved ones, but we still have family that loves us. That alone should be enough. We must be thankful for the things we have and not be bitter for the things we don't."

I thought about it for a minute and I smiled. He was so right. Thanksgiving isn't just about eating a turkey and pumpkin pie. It is a special time to be thankful. And I was fortunate to have my children, my family, my friends and a roof over our heads. And I was also thankful for my new widower friend who knew exactly how I felt! I was lucky to have him to talk with late at night about certain fears that not too many other people would understand. Watching him raise his son alone, and still want to make a life for himself encouraged me to want to do the same. This man would become a very important part of my healing process. He would help me move on with my grief by encouraging and listening to me. We laughed and had so much fun together. He gave me the self-confidence I needed to move forward. He helped me more than he knows. I will cherish our special relationship forever.

That Thanksgiving was the first holiday without my husband that I was actually able to enjoy and it felt good! As I sat around the Thanksgiving table with my children and other various family members, I did manage to smile and when I did, I thought about what my new friend said and secretly whispered a thankful prayer for everything I did have. I noticed that when the Christmas season began, I actually took an active part in shopping and wrapping presents and planning the dinner. I was on my way to feeling normal.

WANTING TO GO ON

◆

With the anticipation of a teenager and the fear of a deer jolting across a busy highway, you forge ahead and decide to accept an invitation to lunch, dinner and maybe even a movie with someone of the opposite sex.

So now comes the day, when someone makes your heart flutter and thoughts are no longer totally on grief, but going on.

With the anticipation of a teenager and the fear of a deer jolting across a busy highway, you forge ahead and decide to accept an invitation to lunch, dinner and maybe even a movie with someone of the opposite sex. The first time this occurs, you may feel very out of place sitting next to a stranger other than your spouse. You will unintentionally compare habits, clothes, cologne scent, and yes, hopefully kisses. You might be inclined to hurry and get into a relationship as quickly as possible because you will want that partnership and "normal" life back immediately. And the loneliness becomes unbearable. We somehow think that if we do not have a member of the opposite sex by our side that we are not "normal."

Take your time. Get to know who you really are now, because you are not the same person as you once were. Everyone has something different to teach us. Learn from all of them. Don't settle for someone just because you don't want to be alone. Be certain this new person brings you joy and pleasure as well as love.

I was very fortunate. The first man I became involved with was another widower who lost his wife in the same airplane crash. We met four months after the crash and became instant buddies. We talked constantly about the plane crash and traded stories about my husband and about his wife. No other man or woman could have put up with our grief. There were times when we would talk on the telephone all night until five in the morning about the hounding of the media, the N.T.S.B. hearings, and exchanging stories about our pasts.

Sometimes we would talk about our fears for our future, and the plans we had made with our spouses. There were many times when I would call him and I could tell by the sound of his voice that he was having a "bad time" and there were many days when he would call me right in the middle of one of my "bad moments."

We understood one another and were gentle and kind with our feelings. We cried together many times, but we also managed to laugh again. We were safe with one another because we were both grieving and not ready for anything else but a special friendship and we were very careful not to cross over the line. We did not want to lose our special friendship. Both of us agreed it was too early. We helped each other through that first year when nobody else in this world could.

One particular night, eight months after the airplane crash, I finally realized that my husband was on that airplane and there was no more hope of mistaken identity or delusions of amnesia. It was the closure I should have had eight months before. I finally received a letter that I requested from the coroner describing what they found of my husband and in very graphic details the description of the way the airplane crashed and the results of what happens when such G-forces crash into the earth at such a high speed. It was gruesome and painful, but something I needed to know to have closure.

It was this man, my dear friend, who allowed me to scream at the top of my lungs towards the sky while he held onto my arms and let me cry into his shoulders. Words flew out of my mouth that night that I still don't remember saying. I was angry at the airlines, angry with my husband for leaving me, angry with God, and angry with myself for being angry! I felt such pain for my poor husband to have had to endure such a tragic abrupt ending to a wonderful, peaceful, loving life. Where was justice? He was a good man. We were a good family. Why us?

It was this man who held my hand tightly for several hours because I was afraid to go to sleep. When I closed my eyes I had nightmarish pictures of the plane crash flashing through my mind. And when I woke up in the middle of the night out of breath, it was he who patted my back and still held onto my hand. And it was this man who woke me up in the morning with his rendition of several Monty Python skits complete with English accent and made me laugh so hard. I forgot about the grief, even if it was for a just a short while.

I remember coming to his rescue several times also. We were each other's support system. This man taught me to not be afraid to do things alone. He helped me to become an independent woman that first year without my husband. He opened my mind to Europe, to Enya, and to cold German beer. We will have this bond forever and he will always hold a special place in my heart.

The second special man who entered my life sauntered into it like a poetic angel on a musical cloud, exactly one year after my husband's death.

He presented me with single long stemmed red roses, poetic love letters and adorable greeting cards. He cooked me gourmet romantic candlelit dinners. He took me on fun romantic rides through the country talking about our life's desires, our dreams, and where we saw ourselves down the road. We both seemed to be unsure of what the future held for us. He would gaze at me in amusement as I endlessly chattered away, always giving me his undivided attention. When we were together it was as though no one else in the world around us existed. We were our own captive audiences.

He made me laugh. He made me want to live again. He allowed me to feel like a woman when I thought those feelings were gone forever. Knowing I was still raw from widowhood, he had the patience of a saint. I was not sure if I was ready to date yet. One year was not all that long. What would people think? Would they think I was over my husband already? That certainly was not the case. Should I stay in the house for yet another year until it was socially acceptable to date? What is the proper time limit before a widow's life becomes her own and she can say she is single again? I asked my children first and foremost. Being teenagers and resuming their own lives they said they were all for me going on with mine too. They were tired of watching me stay home alone every night.

All I knew was that I enjoyed talking with this new man who continued to call me on the telephone to talk about wild talk show guests. We would make these humorous bets, which I always seemed to lose. Being with him brought joy, laughter and such a spark to my life. He was a challenge. But then, so was I.

However, maybe it was too soon for me. Maybe I still needed more healing time before I could possibly take on such a responsibility as love. I wasn't strong yet. I still didn't have my self-confidence back. Maybe he was not the right person for me for the long term. But this man was the right person for me at that moment. He was what I needed at that time in my totally turned-up-side down life. I believe he was sent to enter my world for certain reasons. And I have come to understand why he couldn't stay.

Even though we had such an amusing witty repartee' together, sparks flew constantly whenever we disagreed. Which was most of the time. The humorous banter was part of our bond. We fought with such oomph and such fervor that our blood was at a constant boiling point. But so was our passion for one another. And although passion can be a good thing, the constant disagreeing would never work for a peaceful lifetime with one another. The odds were against us.

I needed someone more conventional, someone who could compliment my life. The Yin and Yang didn't apply with us because we were equally too much alike. We were either Yin or both Yangs at that same time. Although some may think that would be a harmonious attribute to a relationship, it wasn't with us. I needed someone who was different than me but on the same page of the same chapter in the same book. A lifetime together wasn't in the cards for us.

However, this man educated me on different cultures and taught me that not everyone has happy fairy tale endings in this world and that was all right. He unveiled to me an intoxicating, sacrificial, inextinguishable type of love. One that I have never experienced before and doubt I ever will again. He not only made it clear to me that I could be loved again, but he showed me that I could love again as well. He will always be inside my heart no matter what path I take. I will forever be grateful to him for bringing life back into mine.

I tried dating several other divorced men but it didn't work. They were coming out of a bad marriage. I was coming out of a good one. While I listened to them criticize their ex-wives, I didn't have the heart to share my wonderful experiences with my marriage. I couldn't pretend my life with Steve wasn't a happy one or that it never existed. These men really didn't have the patience to hear about the husband who was placed high upon the pedestal. I realized for me, that I needed to find a widower with children.

Did I compare any of these men to my husband at anytime? Of course I did. At times there were similarities with each of them and my husband. But then again, wouldn't I be attracted to what I was attracted to before? Was I looking for Steve through any of them? I suppose I was looking for what I had with Steve, because it was so right for me. But I knew now he was gone. I had come to the conclusion that no matter who I dated or fell in love with again, the important element was to just be myself and not look for what I once had but experience different people and learn from each of them. I could take my time: I didn't need to rush into anything.

A very wise older widow who I volunteered at the hospital with once looked at me and said, "I know you are in a lot of pain right now, but someday, the pain will ease and you will realize that being alone isn't ALL bad! There will be some things that you will secretly appreciate!" As time went on, I found that I could talk long distance on the telephone for four hours and not have to explain it to anyone. It made me feel very independent! And to be able to come and go as I pleased and not worry about running home to cook dinner became a part of my life. I could spend an outrageous amount of money on a sweater and not have to justify it to anyone but myself. All in time I began to realize that she was right. It wasn't all bad. I began to like the person I became. I felt a respect for myself. I was proud of me! I was holding it all together the best way I could. Even though I made mistakes, I learned from them.

I still wanted someone very special to share my dreams, to grow old with, and to hold me tight on a cold night. Whenever I traveled alone or with friends, I looked at loving couples holding hands and longed for that special companionship again. But I no longer had that desperate feeling of being alone for the rest of my life. I was no longer in any hurry. I had faith that if something was supposed to happen, it would. I did not need to settle for anyone unless he was one hundred percent!

As I began to mend and grow from this enlightening, I became more selective. No more dates with self-absorbed men who only talked about themselves. No more blind dates with anybody's idea of their Mr. Right who inevitably turned out to be my Mr. Wrong. If I were going to spend my time with someone, it would have to be someone very special. I was no longer seeking company just for the sake of not being alone. I decided I would rather spend time alone then be with the wrong man. Someone told me that God doesn't close a door without opening a window. I wasn't certain if I believed that there was some grand plan already preconceived and that someday I would understand it all. So many people sent me religious cards about God's tapestry and how there was a reason for everything. I sat home alone many nights waiting for my window to open.

I said a special request prayer to St. Jude to please send me a widower with children. I decided that what I needed was to be with someone who was familiar with what I had experienced. I prayed and wished for a special sensitive widower who would not become insecure if I wanted to talk about my husband with love and pride. Someone with children so he would understand the love I had for my children. Someone whom I could respect, love, laugh with and enjoy his companionship. I needed someone who would still allow me to be independent and at the same time offer to pump my car with gas!

Soon after my special prayer, almost three years after my husband died, when I was just about to give up on happy fairy tale endings and I was certain that I was only entitled to one real true love, the third special man entered my life.

If there truly is an occurrence as "love at first sight," this was it for me. I can honestly say that from the first moment I looked into this man's light blue eyes, bells loudly rang from the highest chapels and fireworks were set off from every corner of the world! I was breathless, speechless and caught totally off guard. He thought by my very stiff reaction that I didn't like him. Quite the opposite. I was just too stunned to react. I don't know what it was, but something spiritual whacked me in the head when I first stared into his eyes. I was mesmerized. It was almost as though our minds were communicating before our mouths had a chance to say a word. There was a special connection. The more we talked the more I realized that there was something very extraordinary going on between us.

His wife also died young and suddenly, of a brain aneurysm, leaving him a single father with the same feelings of loneliness and helplessness that I experienced. He had three beautiful pre-teenage daughters.

Listening to his tragic story broke my heart. I was compelled to meet his daughters. I knew I could help them. I knew I would be able to understand their pain and loss. But more than that, I knew I could fall in love with this man because there was something about his eyes that was so very familiar to me.

There were still traces of pain, loneliness and confusion behind them. Yet there was this little glimmer of hopefulness, of wanting to go on with life just like me. I found someone on the same page in the same chapter of the same book. He was the window I had been waiting to open.

For several months we remained just friends talking about our spouses, our children, our lives and our losses. I found myself becoming entangled with his life on a regular basis. We talked almost daily. Finally we had our first real date. It was more romantic than I ever dreamed possible. We brought photo albums of our families and talked about our kids. We had a romantic dinner and then danced to the sweetest music for hours. The first time he kissed me, the warmth of his lips went directly to my heart. I didn't want to pull away. When we parted, I felt a terrible emptiness. I had to see and be with him again. I believed that he wanted a normal happy life again too.

When I met his daughters, I fell in love with them also. Each one was beautiful in their own way. I wanted to help them have a good life. They lost their mother at such a crucial age. There are certain things a daughter that age just isn't comfortable talking about with her father. They needed me.

I could not wait to bring all of our children together.

I knew that he was the man I wanted to spend the rest of my life with. He was gentle and kind yet firm and self-assured. He was smart and dependable, and I felt safe again. We had such fun and laughed together. Most important is that because we both experienced such terrible losses and loneliness, we realized how short life really was and learned not to take each other for granted. We both agreed to live life to the fullest with pleasure and love.

It was wonderful to have someone special again to share conversations and to make future plans with. I believe we are both the missing pieces of the puzzles in our lives. He is the kind of man I want to grow old with, share grandchildren with, and travel to all the places I wasn't able to go to with my husband.

Our children bonded immediately. Even though there was an age difference, my two got a thrill out of having younger kids around and his three liked having the older two to take them places. They had a common bond. Each one lost a parent. And they had to deal with their remaining parents falling in love!

When you risk your heart, there is a concern of being hurt. Can I do this again? How do I trust? Can I watch the man I love go off to work and not wonder if he will return safely? Will that fear ever fade? If he is late, will I constantly wonder if there was another accident? I still have an enormous amount of fear of loss to deal with. But as I stated earlier, a star filled sky at night just isn't the same unless it is shared. I wanted that normal lifestyle back again. It was just going to take time. And time was something I no longer could afford to waste.

I realized that losing a spouse didn't mean the end of the world. Only the end of that particular world. Falling in love again did not mean I loved my husband any less. It meant that I was capable of loving again. I was just doing as my Uncle Jack suggested. I was "adding on." It was now up to me to make a whole new life. As difficult as it was, I needed to think of it as a new adventure. A new beginning. I had to take many deep breaths and throw away the anger and the bitterness.

I still believe in fairy tale endings and stardust and moonbeams and I know that if this man and I decide to have a future together, there is a chance that I may get hurt, that I may lose again. But if I were to do nothing but sit here and grieve for my husband, paralyzed by fear for the remainder of my life, thinking about what used to be, instead of what could still be, I would be wasting my life. I know Steve would not have wanted that for my children or me. I needed to see past my own grief and realize that people die everyday. People go on every day. I had a choice to make. I wanted to go on.

WHAT I HAVE LEARNED

◆

I will never understand why this tragedy happened to us, and I have learned that I have no other choice but to accept it.

What I have learned from this tragedy is that I am a survivor. I do have the ability to continue living my life even though the path I originally had chosen was now somewhat altered. I have learned that by talking to others who have experienced the loss of a spouse and seeing that they were able to laugh again, live again and sometimes even love again, I was encouraged to do the same. People fall in love and remarry all of the time. If it were not possible, then this world would be full of bitter, sad, and lonely people. And that is just not true. We are all capable of determining our happiness, whatever it may be.

After all of this time, I tell everyone that if Steve were to somehow come back to life, he would look at me and notice all of the changes and wonder what happened to his little "wifey!" What would he think?

Truthfully, after the initial shock of learning that I had traveled to Europe, Bermuda and the Bahamas without him, bought a new car on my own, invested in the stock market, and remodeled the house to my taste, I think he would turn to me and ask me what happened. I would proudly report to him that it was called "survival."

Would he be proud of me? Would he be impressed? Would he even admire my spunk? You bet he would. And I think he might even be a little intimidated!

Yes, I would probably relinquish certain duties back to him, but certainly never again would I relinquish it all. It took me too long to learn what I have learned to do on my own. The man who comes into my life must be extremely secure to allow me to continue with my independence.

I am proud of the fact that I can balance my own checkbook to the penny, pump my own gas, (although I dread that the most) fill my own wiper fluid, pay my own bills, carry my own luggage and understand the difference between stocks and mutual funds. I can use the outdoor grill just as well as any man. I know how to change a furnace filter and I am no longer afraid of driving on the interstate or on the turnpike and I even learned how to master a map. I am not saying that I don't enjoy being treated like a lady. I adore being a passenger on a road trip and I feel very special when a man brings me roses and opens the door for me. It is just that now; I am also capable of doing those things for myself too!

I have had to learn how to adjust, simplify, modify, accept, and depend on myself. I do not know if I could surrender my entire life again the way it used to be when there were two of us living as one. I do not think I can ever again trust that anything is forever. Because I know now that it is not. I have learned that I will never understand why this tragedy happened to us and I have learned that I have no other choice but to accept it.

I have learned that I am a lucky woman to have had such a perfect love. We had what most people spend a lifetime seeking and never find. And for us it came so easily. We fell instantly in love and lived a wonderful life together for twenty years and had two beautiful children. For that I will always be grateful.

I don't like being rushed through life. Sometimes it's the journey that is more educational and exciting then the actual destination. I really try not to sweat the small stuff. I don't have the time or the energy to waste.

When I am with people who have never experienced a death or a tragedy and something small goes wrong, I try to calm them down and make them see how little these problems really are within the big realm of life.

I have also learned that we are on this earth on borrowed time, some a little longer than others. When the time comes to leave this life and you go to whatever God you choose to believe in, it is not going to matter how much money is in your 401K, or the size of your diamond decorating your finger or how many cars you owned at the time of your death. God is going to question you and there is no fooling this Supreme Being because he is already going to know the answer. He is going to ask if you did the best you could with what you had. Did you help people? Were you kind? Were you honest? Did you stop and smell those flowers every time or did you hurry through life because of deadlines and unimportant commitments? Did you appreciate your life on earth enough to be thankful that you lived?

I see the world differently now. When I take a walk, I inhale the fresh air breathing deeply and exhaling with such exuberance. I stare into the sky and appreciate the magnitude and warmth of the bright sun.

The trees contain many more shades of green and the colors of the flowers are much more vibrant. I really do take the time to stop and smell those roses and I draw the scent in slowly as though I am imprinting the bouquet in my memory bank. My senses are more alert now. I listen to the birds singing as they fly over me, watching them in amusement as they tilt their heads and move through life as though nothing in this world really matters.

I try to make shapes out of the puffy white clouds still searching for a spiritual sign from my husband. I follow the cloud until it breaks apart and disappears. I stop and watch the ducks in the pond near my home and smile as they splash with such fervor. I only wish everyone could see how precious we are without experiencing all of the pain and loss. I've found the secret to life. Its called living. And it is the most beautiful experience.

Last of all, I have learned that all of the love poems and beautiful cards and romantic songs that profess a love that will last forever, no longer hold true for me. Nothing really lasts forever. We must appreciate one another now and enjoy our life today. Because for some of us, tomorrow may never come.

For everything there is a season and a time for every purpose under Heaven...

Ecclesiastes 3:19

A time to grieve...
And a time to go on...

Joanne Shortley-Lalonde

Epilogue

◆

On February 14th 1999, in a small quaint white chapel, loud bells echoed powerfully through the bluest skies over Nashville, Tennessee. The young widow and the young widower exchanged marriage vows in front of five smiling happy children (two were hers and three were his). Also in attendance were their immediate families.

She glided down the aisle holding onto the arm of her older brother while the soft music of Pachebel's Cannon in D filled the room. This time, when the camera's flashed, a wide smile appeared upon her face. This was the happy occasion she prayed for, wished upon stars for, and threw pennies into fountains for. As she approached the alter, she saw tears of pride and happiness in the eyes of her handsome fiancé. When their eyes met, they each smiled assuring one another that their lonely days were over. She would once again lavish in that precious title of "wife."

Amongst sniffles from the guests, (tissues for tears of joy this time), a little older, a little wiser, and a lot more seasoned, the Widow Shortley promised once again to love, honor and cherish, till death.

This would be the beginning of Chapter One, Book Two. Cinderella met her Prince Charming…again. Two families become one. The Castle is back in normal running order. Fairy Tales do come true…if you believe.

Afterword

◆

STEPHEN MICHAEL SHORTLEY

I met Steve Shortley at a bus stop two weeks before Christmas when we were both sixteen years old. It was the magical holiday season and the weather was quite frigid. I noticed that this young boy was cute, sweet, and funny. He instantly stole my heart with his sense of humor. Because he made me laugh, I forgot about the freezing temperatures. His eyes sparkled as he spoke to me. Many years later he told me that he fell in love with me immediately.

To describe my husband in a few words, I would have to say he was a genius of a man. He was an honest person, always teaching us to do the right thing. He was a wonderful son, a great father and a loving husband. He appreciated a good joke and groaned at bad ones. He loved a challenge. He loved animals and nature and science fiction movies. His favorite color was blue, favorite author was Stephen King, favorite hero was Clint Eastwood, favorite rock groups were ZZ Top, Led Zeppelin, The Doobie Brothers and Grand Funk Railroad. His favorite candy bar was a *Snickers* and his favorite cookies were *Oreo Double Stuffed*. He loved his family, he adored his children and he loved me. No matter what happened in our lives, our love was a constant.

When I married this young man at the tender young age of eighteen, it never occurred to me that he was super intelligent and going to become a successful executive someday. It didn't matter. I loved him through the hard times as well as the good times. We struggled together financially through the years of college, working full-time and raising children. We dreamed the same dreams and most of them came true. I loved him for better or worse, through sickness and in health, for richer and poorer and I will still love him even after death.

About the Author

◆

Joanne Shortley-Lalonde is now remarried and the proud mother of five children. She has a full busy life again living in Kentucky. She has written several articles for newsletters, newspapers and magazines. Her second book will be her depiction of suddenly becoming a step-mother trying to find a politically correct way to replace that archaic implication that "stepmother" means evil. She still believes in fairy tales and happily-ever-after endings.